Sun Kinks and Saw Byes

SUN KINKS AND SAW BYES

Practising Transportation Law in the Canadian West in the Eighties

PETER W NOONAN

MAGISTRALIS

Ottawa, Canada

Sun Kinks and Saw Byes: © 2012 (2025) by Peter W. Noonan. All Rights Reserved

ISBN (hardcover): 978-1-7780030-7-3

For Cataloguing in Publication Data refer to:

Library and Archives Canada

395 Wellington St., Ottawa, ON K1A 0J1

Canada

DEDICATION

For Peter Chandler Noonan & Shelby Alexandra Noonan

CONTENTS

PROLOGUE ix

PART I. INTRODUCTION

1. Chapter 1 - A UNIQUE PRACTICE 3
2. PIERCING THE CORDILLERA 23

PART II. RAIL LINE RATIONALIZATION

3. THE LAST WHISTLE 37
4. BRANCH LINE EXPERIMENTS 71
5. URBAN RELOCATIONS 88

PART III. THE END OF THE CROWSNEST PASS FREIGHT RATE

6. SHADOWS OF THE PAST 99
7. THE VARIABLE RATE BATTLES 115

PART IV. PASSENGER SERVICES AND NORTHERN ISSUES

8. INTO THE SUNSET 133
9. THE NORTH 155

PART V. MISCELLANEOUS CASES

10. ODDS AND ENDS 169

PART VI. CLOSING ARGUMENTS

11. A WIDER VIEW 183
EPILOGUE 193
Appendix 1 - THE GRAIN CAR ALLOCATION SYSTEM CIRCA 1980'S 196
Appendix 2 - THE TECHNOLOGY AND RESOURCES OF A REGULATORY LEGAL PRACTICE IN THE EIGHTIES 198

PROLOGUE

I was born in 1956 and grew up in Essex County, in the extreme southwestern corner of Ontario. Essex County is sometimes called the sun parlour of Canada owing to its moderate climate relative to most of the rest of the country. I lived in a working-class family – my father was a distillery worker at Hiram Walker and Sons and my mother was a homemaker, except for a brief period in the mid-sixties when she worked in neighbouring Detroit, Michigan. I had one sibling – a younger sister – and through the sixties, we attended Marlborough Public School in West Windsor. However, our parents moved us outside the city into the county in the seventies. We lived in Belle River where I attended Belle River District High School. I graduated from Grade 12 in 1974.

I then sought and obtained admission to a special program at Wilfrid Laurier University in Waterloo, Ontario. A grade 12 graduate who attended the summer session program at Wilfrid Laurier, and who obtained at least a B average in two first-year university courses, would be admitted directly to first-year university bypassing both Grade 13 and the qualifying year in place of Grade 13 which was then offered at several Ontario universities. I was successful in the summer program and I was admitted to first-year university at Wilfrid Laurier University in the autumn of 1974.

My ambition for many years had been to become a lawyer and I wished to enter law school as quickly as possible. However, applicants to Ontario law schools were required to possess a bachelor's degree or to complete two years of regular university before applying. (There was also a requirement to take an aptitude test known as the Law School Admissions Test, or LSAT for short.) I took extra courses in the regular and summer sessions so that I was able to complete a general Bachelor of Arts degree with a major in history and a minor in Anthropology in eighteen months.

Thereafter I applied to several law schools in Ontario, and other provinces, and I was successful in obtaining admission at a number of them. However, for reasons of convenience, I elected to attend the University of Windsor Law School because I could live at home with my parents while attending law school and thus save costs.

Windsor Law School proved to be a good choice for me. My professors were very approachable and relations between students were good. My law school years were largely a blur but I did develop a strong interest in public law courses and took as many of them as I could. I graduated from law school in the spring of 1979 and then stayed in Windsor to complete my year of practical training under articles of apprenticeship at a small general practice law firm.

After one year of articling a candidate for the Bar was required to spend six months from the beginning of September until the end of the following February attending courses and writing examinations in the Bar Admission Course offered by the Law Society of Upper Canada. Students had a choice of whether to attend the Bar Admission Course at facilities in London, Ottawa or at the historic seat of the Law Society at Osgoode Hall in Toronto. I decided that attending the Bar Admission Course at Osgoode Hall would be a valuable experience.

Osgoode Hall is a magnificent building and it occupies a historic position in the legal profession in Ontario and elsewhere in Canada that can be traced back to the eighteenth century. Mornings at Osgoode Hall were spent in large classrooms attending lectures offered by some of the most eminent practitioners at the Bar, followed by small group seminars led by local practitioners who were in the course of establishing their professional reputations. In the afternoon we were free to engage in our private studies. I liked to study upstairs in the Great Library – a magnificent high-ceilinged room with tall windows and architectural highlights. A massive fireplace was located at one end of the room with a clock on the mantelpiece. In the evenings the ticking of the clock echoed in the silence of the chamber. At the far end of the Great Library was a memorial to the Society's losses in the Great War. The tall windows were etched with the initials of Queen Victoria (VR). It was a place that exuded legal history and the gravity of the profession. I was successful in my Bar examinations and it was a proud moment for my family and me when I took the oath of allegiance to the Queen and the oaths of a Barrister and of a Solicitor on April 10, 1981, and thereupon took my place at the Ontario Bar as a member of the Law Society of Upper Canada.[1]

---

1. The day before I had come up to Toronto by train from my parent's home in Windsor to return to Osgoode Hall and sign the official roll of solicitors maintained by the Law Society of Upper Canada.

The author as a newly minted barrister and solicitor in 1981

I was still uncertain about what I wanted to do with my legal education and I spent the better part of the spring and summer of 1981 thinking about my future. While reflecting on what kind of legal practice would inspire me, I recalled my strong interest in public law courses in law school and my fascination with the relationship between law and public policy. Public law influences the development of society and I wished to use my skills in a balanced or neutral capacity to represent and advance the interests of society as a whole, rather than as a partisan advocate. Government practice held out the possibility of a legal career along those lines. I decided that I would seek a career as a government lawyer.

I obtained a copy of the Canadian Almanac and Directory and identified the General Counsel or head of legal services in many federal departments and agencies. I then wrote to them inquiring if they had any vacancies which is how I found myself in an interview with Gilbert W. Nadeau QC and Jean Patenaude in

September 1981 at the offices of the Canadian Transport Commission (CTC) in Hull, Quebec, opposite the Parliament in Ottawa.

My interview with them went well. Jean Patenaude explained that the Commission was hiring a lawyer to assist him at the CTC's Western Division in Saskatoon, Saskatchewan. I was asked if I had any impediments to relocating to Saskatoon and since I had nothing to hold me in the east I told them that I would have no problem relocating to Saskatchewan. At the time I knew very little about Saskatoon but I was young and open to new experiences. Mr. Nadeau seemed relieved that I had no objections to being considered for a job in Saskatoon. Not many local candidates in the Public Service in Ottawa were interested in such an opportunity in the West.

About three weeks after my interview with the CTC I was informed in a telephone call with Mr. Nadeau that I was the successful candidate. He told me to stand by for instructions and that he would get in touch with me in due course. I soon learned that due course actually meant a long time since seven weeks passed before I heard again from the CTC. This time it was Jean Patenaude who called me in late November and asked me to report to him in Saskatoon in early December. I learned subsequently that in the public service, very little in the field of staffing could be done quickly, as a blizzard of paper was required to fill a vacancy. Alas, despite many subsequent reforms over the next thirty years I never found the hiring process to improve to any significant degree.

In the early eighties, the Canadian Transport Commission remained the oldest and largest regulatory agency of the Federal Government, tracing its origins back to the Board of Railway Commissioners for Canada established in 1904. The CTC had incorporated the successor of the Board of Railway Commissioners, the Board of Transport Commissioners for Canada, as well as the former Air Transport Board, and the former Canadian Maritime Commission.

The Commission was headed by a President who was usually a former cabinet Minister. In 1981 when I joined the Commission it was a former Liberal Finance Minister, Edgar Benson, who served as its President. The Commission was divided into two halves, a regulatory section that was headed by the Commission's Vice President – Law, and a research section headed by the Commission's Vice President – Research. Almost all of my activities would be concerned with the regulatory side of the Commission, which was then headed by Vice President Guy Roberge QC, who was soon to be replaced by John Gray QC. The regulatory half of the Commission was organized into separate modal committees oriented to particular modes of transportation. The commissioners (of whom there were more than a dozen) were scattered among the various modal committees. The CTC's committees consisted of the Railway Transport Committee, the Air Transport Committee, the Water Transport Committee, the Motor Vehicle Transport Committee, and the Commodity Pipelines Transport Committee. There was also a small International Transportation Policy Committee that rarely met. Finally, there was a separate Review Committee, consisting of the chairs of the various committees, that acted as an in-house appeal committee hearing administrative reviews of Commission decisions where it was alleged that new facts or changed circumstances had arisen since the date of a modal committee decision, or that a decision was tainted by an error of law or a breach of natural justice.

The vast bulk of the Commission's regulatory work was performed by the rail and air committees and my work would be focussed in those areas, especially in rail transportation. The water committee had limited responsibilities for international shipping cartels, the coasting trade, and northern inland barge services, while the Motor Vehicle Transport Committee mostly processed individual permissions for trucking companies to operate on Sundays under the *Lord's Day Act*[2]. The Committee concerned with commodity pipelines was mostly moribund, as there were few non-oil and gas pipelines to regulate.

Onto this structure, the government in the late seventies and early eighties grafted a hybrid organization known as the CTC Western Division to deal with the pressing issues of the western rail network. Two commissioners from western Canada, James M. McDonough, and Bernard R. Wolfe, were placed in Saskatoon with an administrative and technical staff to alleviate the political pressure that would be felt in Ottawa if decisions on the future configuration of the western rail network continued to be issued from the capital. The CTC Western Division was given the Commission's regional responsibilities for deciding railway branch line abandonment applications as well as some local passenger train discontinuance applications. It also received an operational program from the Department of Transport to conduct inspections and audits of railway capital subsidies under the Prairie Branch Line Rehabilitation Program, a program that was intended to upgrade branch lines that were to be retained as part of a permanent western grain transportation network. The CTC Western Division was also responsible for two satellite offices that dealt with the efficient movement of rail cars used in grain service through the major western grain ports of Thunder Bay, Ontario, Churchill, Manitoba and Vancouver, and Prince Rupert, British Columbia. A limited commercial air service licensing program was also added to the mix.

Throughout the decade from the end of the 1981 until the end of 1991 I served as the legal advisor for that organization. This is my account of that period.

---

2. *Lords Day Act*, R.S.C. 1970, c. L-13

PART I.

INTRODUCTION

CHAPTER 1.

CHAPTER 1 - A UNIQUE PRACTICE

As 1981 gave way to 1982, a significant change took place in the CTC Western Division. Jean Patenaude, our Senior Counsel, left the Commission to join the legal department at Via Rail Canada Inc., in Montreal. His departure placed me in charge of the CTC Western Division legal office and brought me into a close working relationship with the resident quorum of the Commission in Saskatoon, Senior Commissioner J. M. McDonough, and Commissioner B.R. Wolfe.

When I became solely responsible for the legal functions of the CTC Western Division in February 1982, I was 25 years old and still quite green. There had been no time to train me adequately and indeed there was no formal orientation or training program. However, Jean Patenaude had set aside some time from his busy schedule to brief me on what I would be expected to do after he departed. It was with some trepidation that I entered upon what was essentially a sole practice as a regulatory lawyer for the federal government but fear of failure is a great motivator in such circumstances. I took home whatever legal resources I could find, or acquire, concerning transportation law, and railway law in particular, and I read voraciously in the evenings.

Administrative law had always been a strength of mine in law school, and that helped me considerably. I was very conscious of the fact that I had better not fail. Any legal failures in the CTC Western Division would fall on my head since neither of the Western Division commissioners were legally trained. It was difficult at first, and I had a lot of responsibility but I was of an independent mind and I was determined to be seen as a competent legal practitioner. I approached my tasks with diligence and perseverance.

I was not entirely without support because the CTC Western Division was part of a national regulator and there was a full legal services department at the Commission's headquarters in Hull, Quebec. The Commission employed 16 lawyers but I was the only lawyer who was based outside of the National Capital Region. Owing to the need to bring me into the Saskatoon office as quickly as possible there had been no time for me to visit our headquarters and it was not until 1983 that I was able to travel to Ottawa and meet with the other lawyers who the Commission employed.

During my initial year of practice, I occasionally telephoned lawyers of the same rank as myself at CTC headquarters if I was particularly unsure about an issue. Contact with the more senior lawyers in the Commission's legal branch was generally sporadic at best. Nominally, I reported to the General Counsel of the Commission. Still, often many months would elapse without any direct contact between us. However, I was always careful to send him my litigation reports concerning appeals and judicial reviews, as the Commission centrally managed its external litigation. Each modal committee of the Commission had a team of lawyers attached to it and each team was headed by a Senior Counsel who exercised functional responsibility for the legal work of that committee. My contact with the Senior Counsel of the committees was intermittent and usually took the form of a memorandum or a telex. The reasons for the lack of close coordination reflected an intention by the creators of the CTC Western Division that the division should function as much as possible as a separate entity that was autonomous from the main organization, and it should develop its own methods for handling the controversial regional transportation issues for which it was responsible. The consequence for me was that I was essentially on my own as a federal legal practitioner. There were both pros and cons to this arrangement, both for the organization and for me, professionally and personally.

One consequence of being a sole practitioner is that my holidays were more difficult to take than if I had been part of a larger legal team. Although I was allotted three weeks of annual holidays, it was not practical for me to take extended holidays since there was no one to replace me. In later years when I had gained more experience, I was able to plan vacations around major events so that I departed during a quiet time and I was able to arrange for lawyers in the headquarters office to take telephone calls from our western staff if there was an urgent need for legal advice. In other years, when I did not travel, I took a week or ten days at Christmas but remained in touch with the office by telephone. My unused vacation days were paid out to me in cash after the end of the government's fiscal year.

At the outset of my sole practice, I quickly discerned that to be successful in this role I had to earn the confidence of three people, our General Counsel, Gilbert W. Nadeau QC at Commission headquarters, and the two Western Division commissioners, Jim McDonough and Bernie Wolfe, especially the former in his capacity as the Senior Commissioner of the Division. Earning their confidence became an immediate personal goal.

James (Jim) McDonough was an intelligent and driven man with a great deal of knowledge and experience in the grain handling and transportation field. He was a career civil servant who had worked his way up through the federal agriculture bureaucracy. Commissioner McDonough was a very determined man and I appreciated his talents and enjoyed working with him. He had previously served as the Executive Director of former Supreme Court Justice Emmet Hall's Grain Handling and Transportation Commission and he remained on good terms with Mr. Hall. Mr. McDonough had an excellent grasp of agricultural and transportation policy. As the eighties progressed, however, Commissioner McDonough began to suffer from multiple sclerosis, an insidious disease that was unnaturally prevalent in Saskatchewan residents. He displayed great courage in continuing to discharge his duties while his health deteriorated, an effort of willpower that impressed everyone who came into contact with him. After the Commission was wound up at the end of 1987, he continued for one year as a Member of the National Transportation Agency but his health no longer permitted him to attend the office regularly and he retired from office at the end of 1988.

Senior Commissioner James M. McDonough disembarking from a Beechcraft King Air aeroplane

Bernard (Bernie) Wolfe was of a different character. He had risen to prominence through municipal politics in Winnipeg and organized politics held great interest for him. When I first met him, I committed the faux pas of saying that I understood that he had been Deputy Mayor of Winnipeg under long-time Winnipeg Mayor Stephen Juba. He fixed me with a glowering stare and said; "I was Deputy Mayor of Winnipeg UNDER no one!" Afterwards, I was a lot more circumspect when discussing that subject with him! Bernie Wolfe was a people person and he took to heart the view that all politics were local. Although he grasped policy well enough, he was more interested in how policy, and particularly government policy on rail line abandonments, would affect ordinary Canadians. Thus while Commissioner McDonough had a firm grasp of the macro transportation policy issues facing western Canada in the eighties, Commissioner Wolfe had a strong interest in how the application of policy would affect local residents. In this respect, the two Western Division commissioners proved to have complementary skills for tackling the difficult issues surrounding the grain handling and transportation system in the eighties.

Good relations with my working colleagues in the CTC Western Division were also essential, starting with the Executive Director, John Kimpinski, who had long experience in railway tariffs and tolls gained from his career at the CN where he had begun as a business car clerk. Frequently, I worked with our Directors of Engineering (Ken Tikkanen and later Jim Cant) and our Directors of Rail Operations (initially Martin Lacombe followed later by Bud Ripley)[1]. As legal counsel, I was excluded from collective bargaining as were the directors and with them, I formed part of the management team in the CTC Western Division[2].

1. Many of our employees had experience working on the railways. Members of our technical staff had worked variously on the CN, the CP, Northern Alberta Railways, and the Ontario Northland Transportation Commission railway. Jim Cant had also built railways in southern Africa for the Canadian International Development Agency.
2. At this point in my career I held the lowest rank in the Law Group, the classification of LA-1. A federal lawyer at this level was not regarded as having reached the normal working level and is usually closely supervised by more senior counsel. Under the incumbency-based rules for promotion that applied at that time to government lawyers, I was entitled to be considered for promotion to the working level (LA-2A)

Although I was counsel to the Commission as a whole my role and location meant that it was uncommon for me to deal with the commissioners based at the headquarters of the Commission. Occasionally, I would assist one of them when they were assigned to a western case and some commissioners from Ottawa also served on CTC Western Division hearing panels. Although the quorum of the Commission consisted of two commissioners acting together, it was often thought desirable to have at least three commissioners to hear a case if there was a possibility of a dissent on a panel of two. Commissioner Robert J. Orange served so frequently as our third commissioner that we began to regard him as the "Honourary" third commissioner of the CTC Western Division. Commissioner Orange was an affable man who had been a public servant in northern Canada before being elected as a Liberal Member of Parliament for the Northwest Territories. Later, after serving in Parliament, he was appointed to the Commission. His knowledge of the North was particularly helpful in cases involving northern issues, and I welcomed the opportunities we had to work together.

upon the fifth anniversary of my commencement of service. I received my promotion almost like clockwork in December 1987. Later, when I assumed the responsibilities of a dispute resolution professional in the NTA Western Region I moved into the commerce group (CO) for a few years, as the NTA's dispute resolution work was classified as commercial, rather than legal, work in the public service. I returned to the law group in my later career.

Commissioners Bernard R Wolfe, left, and Robert J. Orange, right, in northern Manitoba

My relationship with the local Bar was not close since my practice areas did not overlap to any great extent with any other lawyer's practice areas in Saskatoon. The local lawyer whose practice was closest to mine may have been Willie Grieve at PURC, the Public Utilities Review Commission, a Province of Saskatchewan regulatory body, and Mr. Grieve and I occasionally discussed broad issues of regulatory law.

One local group that I did take the initiative to meet was the local office of the federal Department of Justice, then located in offices on 4th Ave. South. My Justice colleagues were very welcoming and I did have a purpose in meeting with them. My predecessor Jean Patenaude, a member of the Quebec Bar, had appeared on the radar screen of the Law Society of Saskatchewan and the Secretary of the Law Society, Iain Mentiplay, had questioned Patenaude's right to practise law without a Saskatchewan licence. There had been warnings of strong action to come from the Law

Society and Mr. Patenaude needed to place the issue in the hands of the Department of Justice since the issue involved federal-provincial jurisdiction and the Justice Department lawyers were responsible for such matters.

I did not have any objection in principle to joining the Law Society of Saskatchewan but two factors caused me to oppose it. Firstly, the inter-jurisdictional transfer rules of that era made it difficult to transfer from one provincial bar to another. In my case, I would have been required to undertake new articles of apprenticeship under a member of the Law Society of Saskatchewan and thereafter successfully write the Saskatchewan bar exams. Furthermore, the federal government had agreed to pay the annual licensing fees of government lawyers because the government required its lawyers to maintain a membership in a provincial or territorial bar. However, the government would only pay the fees for one bar association and since I did not know where my career would lead at that early stage I was reluctant to give up my Ontario membership. It would have been a financial burden to pay the Saskatchewan fees, particularly because the Saskatchewan Bar, unlike the Ontario Bar, did not exempt government solicitors from paying for professional liability insurance.

There were two reasons why I thought that we did not require a Saskatchewan licence to act as counsel to the Commission in our Saskatoon location. Firstly, I believed that the principles of inter-jurisdictional immunity that exist between Her Majesty in Right of Canada and Her Majesty in Right of Saskatchewan precluded the province from attempting to stipulate the job requirements of a federal public servant. Essentially, the federal government could hire whomever it pleased and title them in whatever way suited the needs of the federal government.

Secondly, Parliament had explicitly constituted the Canadian Transport Commission as a court of record under the *National*

Transportation Act[3] and Parliament was entitled to create the CTC as an additional court under section 101 of the *British North America Act*[4], which then served as Canada's constitution. Any lawyer who had been called to the Bar in any Canadian province or territory was entitled to practice before a federal court in any part of the country. Therefore, I believed that an Ontario lawyer could appear at hearings and provide internal legal services to a federal court of record that had its office in Saskatchewan.

However, by the time I joined the CTC Western Division, it seemed that the dispute with the Law Society of Saskatchewan had largely run its course and that the Law Society had grudgingly accepted its lack of jurisdiction in the matter. Nevertheless, the Department of Justice counselled me to keep my head down and to avoid any conflicts with the Law Society of Saskatchewan, which was good advice that I followed. I never encountered any difficulties with the Saskatchewan Bar over this issue.

I continued to visit the Justice offices annually as in those days the Law Society of Upper Canada required that our annual practice reports filed with the Law Society be commissioned before a commissioner of oaths. Therefore, I would present myself each year at the Justice Department and have my law society documents commissioned by a Saskatchewan commissioner for oaths employed by the Department of Justice.

In Saskatoon, despite a lack of professional overlap with members of the local bar I did join the Saskatoon Bar Association, a local social and professional organization, and I enjoyed attending some of the functions of the local bar association. The bar association always sent its notices to my office with one exception. An invitation to the annual Winter Ball was always sent to my residence. I asked the Secretary about it one time and I was told that the invitation to the annual ball was always sent to the

---

3. *National Transportation Act*, R.S.C. 1970, c. N-17.
4. *British North America Act*, 30 & 31 Vict., c. 3 (U.K.)

residences of lawyers because male lawyers were notorious for avoiding the Winter Ball and it was hoped that by sending the invitation to a lawyer's private residence his spouse would find out about it and prevail upon him to go to the event!

One notable local bar function involved a visit to Saskatoon of the Minister of Justice and Attorney General of Canada, the Hon. Mark MacGuigan PC MP, in the early eighties. The Saskatoon Bar Association hosted a reception for him at the Saskatoon Club and since he was the senior Law Officer of the Crown in Right of Canada I felt obliged as a federal government lawyer to attend. It was a pleasant occasion and the Minister recognized my name since I shared it with my grandfather whom the Minister knew personally. Much later I learned from my father that MacGuigan had later taken the trouble to mention our meeting to my grandfather. Although the Minister knew nothing about my practice, he assured my grandfather that I was doing an excellent job!

In the mid-eighties the local bar association decided to honour a favoured son of Saskatchewan, the Hon. Emmett Hall, a retired Justice of the Supreme Court. That proved to be a well-attended event, with many prominent counsel as well as judges and former judges in attendance. Emmett Hall and Commissioner McDonough were friends and I sometimes met former Justice Hall whenever he called on the commissioner in our offices. In later years he would sometimes join our senior staff when we attended meetings of the local chamber of commerce. He was a very polite and courtly elderly gentleman who was much admired in Saskatchewan for his work in Medicare and by the Bar for the prominence of his judgements, including his notable judgement in the groundbreaking aboriginal law case involving the Nisga'a First Nation of British Columbia.

My professional relations were naturally strongest with the members of the small railway bar in western Canada since the bulk of my practice involved railway law. Although much of the regulatory work had historically been concentrated at the headquarters of the two major railways in Montreal, the creation of the CTC Western Division caused a large chunk of that regulatory business to be handed off to the western-based counsel of the railways. With the CN I dealt mostly with its Winnipeg-based counsel, primarily Grant Nerbas, Associate General Counsel for regulatory affairs in Western Canada. Grant was a very decent man, whose humanity often shone through at abandonment hearings when the Crown-owned railway became the target of criticism by members of the Public. Grant never overreacted to the comments made by the public no matter how incorrect or unfair those comments might be. In this regard, he was the perfect choice to deflect the slings and arrows directed at the CN as it tried to reduce its infrastructure and costs. He even tried to inject some humour into the abandonment process on occasion. At one hearing a group of grade eight students came to present a brief as a panel of witnesses. When they had spoken, he rose to cross-examine them and asked if they recalled the station sign at the local station. When they affirmed that they knew of it he said that it had recently disappeared, and did they know where the CN might be able to find it? The sheepish look on students' faces gave a moment of delight to the proceedings as it was clear that they all knew something about it. While the bulk of my Canadian National files involved Grant Nerbas in Winnipeg, I did on some occasions deal with other CN lawyers in Edmonton or Vancouver.

Unlike Canadian National Railways, the Canadian Pacific Limited did not concentrate its western regulatory law business in one location, and I would deal variously with Winston Smith and Allan Ludkiewicz in Winnipeg for CP files in Manitoba and Saskatchewan, Marcella Szel and Marc Shannon in Calgary for Alberta files, and Gail Macdonald and Laura Sugimoto in Vancouver for British Columbia matters. The CP was Canada's main private-sector transportation company and in those days it was a large conglomerate consisting not only of a railway but also a major airline (CP Air), a shipping line (CP Ships), a hotel chain, and a telecommunications company. CP counsel were always more businesslike and less relaxed at proceedings than CN counsel. However, they were invariably polite and professional in all of the dealings that I had with them through the years.

On a few occasions, I would deal directly with the office of the General Solicitors of CP and CN in Montreal, Gordon Miller QC at CP, and Serge Cantin c.r. at CN, and for any Via Rail business that I had I would deal with our former CTC Western Division Senior Counsel Jean Patenaude, or another of his colleagues at Via Rail Canada headquarters in Montreal. In the West, I also dealt sometimes with the lawyers for the Burlington Northern Railway Co. which operated some lines into British Columbia and Manitoba. The BN's legal business was handled by Malcolm King of the Vancouver law firm Douglas, Symes and Brissenden and he was always pleasant and professional to deal with.

On the shipper's side, I dealt extensively with Marshall Rothstein QC, Jim Foran QC, and Marc Monnin of the Winnipeg law firm Aikens, MacAulay and Thorvaldson. Without a doubt, Marshall Rothstein was the leading transportation practitioner of the day and he appeared for the large shippers on the major cases of the era. He was bright, tenacious, and thorough. He never left a stone unturned if it needed to be turned over. Hard work was a necessity of practise for him and I never saw a case that he was involved with where he did not have a mastery of his brief. His cross-examinations of witnesses were very penetrating and his arguments were always crafted with great care. He was a leading barrister of the period and he went on to serve on the Federal Court, the Federal Court of Appeal, and eventually on the Supreme Court of Canada. Marc Monnin served as his very able junior in those days and he too would subsequently rise to high judicial office in Manitoba. Jim Foran was a very able barrister whom I saw less of because his practice concentrated more on the trucking side of the transportation business and the Commission and its successor lacked any substantial jurisdiction in the trucking field. One other prominent shipper counsel from those days was Ottawa-based counsel Francois Lemieux, who was also a future judge of the Federal Court, and who often acted for the Province of Saskatchewan in major railway tariff cases.

In rail rationalization cases counsel from the private bar rarely appeared. There were occasional exceptions however and the long regulatory and judicial path required for the abandonment of the CP-CN Langdon Subdivision joint section brought me into extended contact with Robert Ross QC of Drumheller, who proved to be a convivial colleague as that case meandered its way through the review and appeal process. Once, after a Supreme Court appearance in Ottawa, and a pleasant dinner afterwards, a number of the railway counsel and I took up Bob's invitation to tour the hidden treasures of the national aeronautical museum's rarely viewed warehouse collection of aeroplanes and aeronautical artifacts, courtesy of an old friend of Mr. Ross.

My relations with the aeronautical bar were not as close as my relations with the railway bar. The CTC Western Division dealt only with the smaller commercial air services offering charter services. Nevertheless, over time, I had dealings with J. D. Barnsley and Robin Kersey in Winnipeg. Occasionally I would also deal with Peter Wallis, a former Senior Counsel of the Commission, who was at Pacific Western Airlines in Calgary, or with his regulatory affairs associate, Pierre Roy, both of whom proved very helpful over the years in resolving disputes between the carrier and disgruntled passengers.

Appellate practice in the courts was also a focus of my legal practice. I handled the CTC Western Division's appeal and judicial review business and occasionally some Western legal appeals for our Commission headquarters. Special restrictions applied to me as a lawyer for an independent quasi-judicial body. Although the CTC had a statutory right to appear by counsel in any appeal from one of its decisions the role of counsel for the Commission had been considerably circumscribed by jurisprudence. The courts quite rightly took the view that it was unseemly for a quasi-judicial body to enter the fray in an appeal from one of its decisions, and therefore the judges read a restriction into the law that obligated all counsel from a quasi-judicial tribunal to restrict themselves to the role of a 'friend of the court'. In this capacity, I was limited to addressing the court to correct or assist in any matter concerning the record of the proceedings before the Commission, or to address questions of statutory jurisdiction. However, I could not address the court in argument on any aspect of the Commission's conduct in the case, and in particular, I could not answer any complaint about procedural unfairness by the Commission, or a lack of natural justice. Only counsel for the Attorney General of Canada could address the court on those subjects. Therefore, I always had to ensure that any representations I made on behalf of the Commission were balanced, non-partisan, and respectful of the restrictions placed upon counsel for a quasi-judicial body. While a little more latitude was given to tribunal counsel in cases where the tribunal was being subjected to a motion for prohibition to stop its proceedings in the main the courts expected a balanced and circumspect approach from Commission counsel and I always strove to give them that. The judges that I appeared before always treated me with respect and particularly in the Federal Court of Appeal I found I was called upon to assist the judges in understanding the record or chronology of the case.

In appellate advocacy it was my main responsibility to prepare and certify the record of the proceeding, guided by the *Federal Court Rules* and by my best judgement as to what the record should contain. I would therefore assemble all of the documents and transcripts required by the *Federal Court Rules* and after having the Secretary of the Commission certify them to be the originals I would take them down to the registry of the Court of Queen's Bench in Saskatoon which held a cross-appointment as the local registry of the Federal Court Trial Division and the Federal Court of Appeal. There, the local officers of the court would take custody of the documents and arrange for them to be printed and bound in the manner customary in Federal Court practice.

As a matter of practice, whenever the Commission was successful in the Federal Court or the Supreme Court, and legal costs were awarded, I always declined to accept them because I believed that a quasi-judicial body should never impede the efforts of people or organizations that wished to dispute a decision or order and that taking out costs could have such an effect.

I appeared less often in the Supreme Court of Canada than in the Federal Courts and in the Supreme Court, the appeal books that constituted the record were prepared by the counsel having carriage of the appeal, thus relieving me of that burden. However, my usefulness to the court in explaining the record was less in evidence where I was not responsible for the contents of the appeal record. Although I was able to assist the Court on several occasions, my main function in Supreme Court appeals was largely one of standing by if the court sought my assistance on some general question of the Commission's practices. Nevertheless, it is the dream of many lawyers to appear at least once in the nation's highest court and the few occasions upon which I had the opportunity to represent my government client in that forum were a high professional honour.

Naturally, with the heavy emphasis placed on rail rationalization work in the CTC Western Division, I dealt quite often with federal politicians. It was extremely important for a federal Member of Parliament to be seen to actively participate in rail abandonment hearings. I dealt with MPs, or sometimes prospective candidates, at hearings by facilitating their appearances to conform to their schedules. I also had to examine them concerning their evidence but there the expectation was that I would only ask broad questions that allowed them to speak to the rail rationalization issue in broad terms. The politicians, in turn, did their best to focus on community impacts arising from the rationalization process and to avoid overtly partisan comments in their evidence. Outside of hearings I dealt with officials in MP's offices and occasionally with aides to federal ministers, more so after the Progressive Conservative party replaced the Liberals in 1984 probably because there was so much more Western representation in the Progressive Conservative government than in the previous Liberal Ministry. There were occasional gaffes. Once, a New Democratic Party (NDP) MP from Regina, Les Benjamin, stopped by our office late in the day looking for some documents that were accessible to the public. Unfortunately, our support staff had left by that time and together with our Senior Economist, Roy Proctor, I strove mightily and without success to get the office photocopier to work properly. Much chagrined and feeling like a caricature of a bumbling civil servant I had to undertake to send the material to him on the next business day after our support staff returned! It was a lesson that underscored the essential role played by our excellent support staff. They made an efficient legal practice possible.

Rail issues were also very important for provincial politicians and I dealt frequently with them at hearings and at other times. It was not unusual for provincial Members of the Legislative Assembly, even provincial Ministers, to telephone me directly to ask for information. However, as the provinces are a separate level of government provincial politicians and provincial officials were normally not entitled to greater information than was provided to the public. At hearings, provincial politicians also testified on the subject of broad social impacts and the same expectations were placed on me in regards to their testimony as it was in the case of testimony by federal politicians. Ordinarily, I would allow politicians to expound on the broad social changes that were affecting local communities. With the provincial politicians, there could be an edge to their representations based on federal-provincial tensions which were ordinarily overlooked. On one or two occasions, however, I observed provincial ministers making inaccurate statements. Although I was uncertain as to whether those inaccuracies were due to an inadequate briefing by provincial officials or a deliberate strategy, I realized that left unchallenged that could result in those members of the public who viewed the proceedings drawing erroneous conclusions about the evidence. In those situations, I did have to take a firmer line with them in my examination of their testimony. Although inaccurate testimony from a member of the public might not be challenged at a hearing if it was not critical to the accuracy of the record (especially if it consisted of opinion evidence rather than important factual evidence) accuracy and consistency were expected from the provincial governments in their evidence to ensure that the general public would not be misled. In general, however, my many interactions with provincial politicians and provincial officials in the hearing processes were quite cordial.

Relations with the media were also of great importance in my practice. The work of the Western office involved many public issues and it was natural that the media followed them closely. Given that the Commission was a quasi-judicial body it was clear that the commissioners could not discuss any aspect of a pending case with the media. Due to the lack of a communications officer in the CTC Western Division the duty of acting as a media relations person was often assigned to me as the western legal counsel. I dealt with many members of the print and broadcast media over the years and I gave many print and radio interviews as well as some television interviews. I gave so many of them that our local newspaper, the Saskatoon Star-Phoenix, asked me to come down to their offices one day so that they could photograph me for their newsmaker archive. As a lawyer, I had some general professional guidelines for relations with the media in law society and Canadian Bar Association rule books but generally, I followed the simple rule of telling them with accuracy what they wanted to know and advising them candidly when information they wanted could not be divulged. In a legal practice, one must approach media interviews with a great deal of care. I found the quality of the press to be good for the most part. Certainly, for the large daily newspapers or the specialized press such as the Western Producer, where I was frequently interviewed by its transportation reporter, Adrian Ewins, I found a very high degree of professionalism and I was never misquoted. However, I found that it was necessary to be more careful with media that undertook a one-off interview with me, particularly if the interviewer did not have a good grasp of the issues in the first place. In such circumstances, the danger of being misquoted could increase. Radio and television interviews were also more problematic due to the impact of edited tape, and one had to think very quickly and carefully in such interviews. One media tactic I learned to watch for was a brief rehearsal of the interview without tape rolling which appeared innocuous but which was followed by an on-tape interview where a question phrased innocuously in the rehearsal was given a more dangerous spin in the actual interview. Media relations were an aspect of practice that kept me on my toes!

Given the purpose in creating the CTC Western Division relations with the general public remained fundamental to our task. Many of the issues that we dealt with in those years affected people in their communities and feelings and emotions sometimes ran high. That fact that two or three hundred people in a small town might show up to a rail abandonment hearing illustrates that these issues were of great public concern. It was essential to listen patiently to the concerns of the public and to ensure that they received whatever helpful assistance we could provide to enable them to exercise their right to be heard in the hearing process. That meant not only speaking to prospective witnesses before their appearance to explain our procedures but also asking them some public interest questions after they had finished reading their briefs or statements to the commissioners.

Our public hearings were open to anyone to attend and we never arranged for any security even though we knew that emotions might run high. Sometimes in cases on the northern periphery of the branch line network, I would see pick-up trucks pull up to the hearing location with rifles slung in the back windows and that gave one a momentary pause but there was never any trouble and the public seemed grateful that someone from the government had come to their community to listen to them. The key to a successful public hearing was to respect the participants and to help them to participate in the process, which became a special task of mine.

I found that people's emotions ran higher in the few cases in which the Commission adjudicated the construction of new physical facilities than in cases that involved the removal of an existing facility. It seemed that it was often easier for people to accept the loss of something that had been present over a long time than to contemplate a new facility that might potentially affect the quiet enjoyment of their lands even if it provided a social benefit. In one case involving the construction of a new line some of the people least affected became the most upset. One individual in particular remonstrated with me about the proposal and was so agitated that our chief engineer, Jim Cant, came up to me afterwards and said; "Peter, I thought that fellow was going to punch you right in the nose!" But in all such cases, I was able to allay the suspicions of the participants and lower the emotional tempers that were often a normal part of the regulatory process.

Sometimes producers or other members of the public would visit our offices in Saskatoon to express their concerns and our staff always made an effort to ensure that they were welcomed and that one or more of our officers would set aside time to speak to them. We also travelled to public meetings where public transportation issues affecting federal concerns were being raised both to explain federal regulatory processes and to lend our subject-matter expertise where it was warranted. Whenever we travelled to a hearing or public meeting, we knew that we were being carefully assessed and watched by our fellow citizens. Once, when we journeyed a short distance from Saskatoon to Watrous, Saskatchewan, which was about two hours away by car, one old gentleman spoke to our operations director, Bud Ripley saying; "I suppose that you are all out here on full expenses!"

Our engineering staff located in technical offices in Winnipeg, Calgary, and Vancouver, often went into the field to meet with local officials and railway representatives. Those contacts proved fruitful in preventing or ameliorating the potential for disputes to arise. Over time the efforts made in the CTC Western Division and its successor the NTA Western Region helped to restore a positive image to federal decision-making in the transportation sphere, and our public outreach efforts were a key component of that process.

CHAPTER 2.

PIERCING THE CORDILLERA

With a sense of anticipation, I boarded Air Canada's western flight in Windsor on December 8, 1981, for my journey to Saskatoon to commence my law practice as a regulatory counsel for the Canadian Transport Commission, Western Division. When I arrived after dark that evening it was a clear, cold, and crisp night with the city alive in Christmas lights and decorations. I settled quickly into the classic Bessborough Hotel which became my home for the next several weeks. Some time afterwards I secured a downtown apartment. My legal career in the Public Service of Canada was underway[1].

A few days after I arrived in Saskatoon in December 1981, I became engaged in an important regulatory case – an application by Canadian Pacific Limited for permission to construct the Mount Macdonald tunnel through the Selkirk range in the western Cordillera. The tunnel case involved the historic main line of the Canadian Pacific, the crowning engineering achievement of nineteenth-century national government and private enterprise which had provided the essential link between the west and the settled parts of eastern Canada. Traversing the western mountains had always been the most difficult part of constructing and operating the transcontinental railway. The critical part

---

1. Although I arrived in winter – never the best season in Saskatoon I quickly grew to love this beautiful prairie city which has always remained one of my favourite Canadian cities. Apart from the frigid temperatures, two things that immediately impressed me in my first days were that some of the City's police officers still wore buffalo robe winter coats and, unusually at that time, the City had created scramble corners at some major intersections to allow pedestrians to cross diagonally.

of the Pacific Railway was a high pass first believed to exist by Walter Moberly and Albert Perry in the 1860s but not actually discovered until the pioneering surveying work of Colonel A.B. Rodgers, for whom the pass was afterwards named, in 1881.

Rodgers Pass was a mysterious place in the nineteenth century. The indigenous people did not go there, even to sojourn, because winter conditions routinely resulted in great avalanches of snow and rock from the mountains into the valley below. Here, warm and moist Pacific air currents collide with the frigid arctic drafts to annually produce the greatest fall of snow in North America. The construction crews pushing the Pacific Railway through the pass in the mid-1880s feared the environment but initially, the railway company thought it could manage the pass with snow-sheds, pusher engines, and standby crews to clear the snow which fell from the mountaintops in avalanches. However, in 1910 sixty-two men died when an avalanche fell upon a crew attempting to clear the track from an earlier avalanche. The Canadian Pacific realized then that Rodgers Pass could not be safely operated even with precautions and the company decided to go underground. Accordingly, the CPR built the five-mile-long Connaught Tunnel in 1916 to alleviate the hazards of the Pass. However, the grade approaching the tunnel from the east through the Beaver Valley was a maximum of 2.6 percent, which limited the size and tonnage of westbound trains and necessitated the use of pusher engines, thereby creating an inefficient bottleneck that constrained the movement of traffic on Canadian Pacific's main line.

Before the completion of the tunnel pusher engines, like these photographed at Rogers Station, were necessary to move trains over Rogers Pass (photo: JC Cant)

In the 1970s, Canadian Pacific embarked on a massive scheme to lower the grade on its main line through the Selkirks to accommodate the growth of Pacific-bound traffic that was projected to occur in the latter part of the twentieth century. At the time of the tunnel case in 1981, Canadian Pacific had completed three other smaller projects which reduced its controlling grades to one percent, compensated for curvature. Those projects involved track changes between Tappan and Notch Hill on the Shuswap Subdivision near Salmon Arm BC, Clanwilliam on the Shuswap Subdivision near Revelstoke BC, and at Stephen on the Laggan Subdivision near Lake Louise, Alberta, in Banff National Park. This last project had resulted in considerable damage to the landscapes in the park which had not been remediated to the satisfaction of the national park authority and that would lead Parks Canada officials to vigorously contest the forthcoming tunnel project.

This fourth, last, and greatest of the grade reduction projects undertaken by CP was located at Beaver Hill on the approach of the Mountain Subdivision to Rodgers Pass not far from Revelstoke BC, and within the boundaries of Glacier National Park. The tunnel project involved approximately twenty-one miles of new trackage between Rodgers Siding and a point two and one-half miles west of Glacier Station. Initially, it was planned that the new trackage would parallel the existing trackage but it would then diverge to a proposed new one-mile tunnel which would take the railway line under the Trans-Canada highway. After proceeding under the highway, the new trackage would bridge Connaught Creek before entering the east portal of a proposed nine-mile long tunnel having its east portal in Mount Macdonald and its west portal in Mount Cheops. The new tunnel would be three hundred feet below the existing Connaught tunnel and eight hundred and forty feet below the summit of Rodgers Pass. The Rodgers Pass tunnel project was projected to cost five hundred million dollars and was considered to be the largest single construction project undertaken by Canadian Pacific since the completion of the main line of the Pacific Railway in 1885.

This was the setting for my first hearing before the Commission, a hearing that took place in Revelstoke, British Columbia on December 16 and 17th 1981. As befitting the importance of the case, the quorum of the Commission was to consist of the President of the Commission, the Hon. E.J. Benson PC, Commissioner J. T. Gray QC, the Chairman of the Railway Transport Committee of the Commission, and Commissioner McDonough, the Senior Commissioner of the CTC Western Division. Most of the hearing support staff came from our western office in Saskatoon. Somewhat perplexing upon our arrival, however, was the news that President Benson had travelled as far as Edmonton before deciding to return to Ottawa. However, as the legal quorum for the Commission consisted of two commissioners the hearing took place without him, with Commissioner Gray serving as the chairman of the panel.

Canadian Pacific was represented by its Vancouver-based Pacific Regional Counsel, Norman D. Mullins QC, and R. M. McLearn from the railway's Montreal headquarters. Jean Patenaude[2] and I, who acted for the Commission, were the only legal counsel who were present. The main protagonist was Dr. Bruce F. Leeson, a scientist who represented the national parks authority, Parks Canada. An assortment of parks and wildlife authorities, union representatives, and federal and provincial politicians rounded out the cast of participants.

Canadian Pacific presented its proposal to the Commission through its Vice President, J.D. Bromley. The new tunnel was to be a truly massive engineering feat and the company had retained several top consultants to assist with its design and construction. The nine-mile tunnel would be concrete-lined and concrete slabs would be fixed to the floor of the tunnel. The line would be double-tracked and rails would be mounted on pads and held in place by special clips. The tunnel would have a height of twenty-five feet and ten inches and a width varying between seventeen and eighteen feet. But the most significant feature of the tunnel would be the ventilation system. Due to its length, ventilation was an absolute necessity to avoid asphyxiating the crews and shutting down the engines as the trains proceeded through the tunnel.

A 1,145-foot vertical ventilation shaft would be drilled through the mountain to connect to the tunnel below. Steel gates would be constructed at the east portal and mid-tunnel. Powerful fans would be installed atop the ventilation shaft and at the east portal. As a train approached the east portal the gates would be open and the train would pass through the portal into the tunnel. The east portal fans would commence to operate to clear the tunnel of fumes from the engines. As the rear of the train passed the midpoint section, the mid-tunnel doors would close and fans in

---

2. Jean Patenaude was only able to attend the first day of the two-day hearing.

a head-house atop the vertical ventilation shaft would operate to cleanse the western section of the tunnel of fumes, and to bring in fresh air in from the western portal. After the train exited the western portal the mid-tunnel doors would again be opened and the fans would shut down.

From an economic perspective, the railway described the consequences if the company failed to obtain permission to build the Mount Macdonald and Mount Shaughnessy tunnels (the latter was the adjacent one-mile tunnel under the Trans-Canada highway) from the Commission. Canadian Pacific described how traffic over its main line to the port of Vancouver BC had grown between 1965 and 1980 by 236 percent, resulting from a major growth in western Canadian exports of grain, coal, sulfur, and petrochemicals. Traffic forecasts suggested that further substantial growth would occur as demand from Asian markets continued. However, the operational constraints imposed by the controlling grade at this location would limit the ability of the railway to meet the demands of western shippers with consequent economic loss to Canada.

Canadian Pacific pressed upon the Commission the urgency of completing the hearing and obtaining a decision from the Commission. The Commission therefore sat extraordinary hours to complete the evidence. On the first day of the hearing, the Commission sat from ten A.M. until after one A.M. the next morning!

From the outset, the main issue revolved around the environmental impacts of the project, and, in particular, the vertical ventilation shaft. At this time there was no formal process of environmental assessment of infrastructure projects under federal legislation as there later would be. Although the federal government had established an environmental assessment and review process in 1973, that process was established through an order-in-council[3], rather than through a regulation[4], and therefore it was an administrative process rather than a mandatory law of general application. However, the Commission also had a legal mandate to examine environmental issues as a matter affecting the broader public interest, and its decision reflected that jurisdiction.

The main point of environmental contention concerning the ventilation shaft was its location. Since the Mt. Macdonald tunnel was to be constructed in Glacier National Park, the national park authority was very concerned about maintaining the pristine environment of this internationally-known mountain treasure. Within the park, there was a well-known view site marked by crossed arches. From that vantage point, a viewer could see a wonderful vista of snow-capped peaks. So beautiful was that site that the provincial tourism authorities had used it in their marketing of British Columbia as an international tourist destination.

Into this mountain magnificence, Canadian Pacific now proposed to build its vertical ventilation shaft atop which the company would perch a two-story head-house to enclose the powerful ventilation fans and the apertures for the release of diesel fumes. Not only would the head-house be situated in plain view of anyone stopping at the famous mountain viewpoint but in addition black smoke would periodically belch from the head-house as trains passed through the tunnel, activating the ventilation system. The railway maintained that from a geotechnical perspective, the location chosen for the head-house was the best

---

3. An order in council is an order made by the Governor General acting on the advice of the current Ministers of the Government which can have narrow or broad legal effects. In reality, it expresses a decision of the federal cabinet.

4. A regulation is a form of subordinate legislation that is made under an Act of Parliament. It can bind the public as clearly as an Act of Parliament itself. Regulations are generally enacted by the Governor General in Council (effectively the federal cabinet) or by a Minister. Regulations remain subordinate to an Act of Parliament and cannot conflict with an Act. If they do, the Act of Parliament will prevail.

possible location. A prestigious firm of New York architects had been retained to design the head-house. Amongst the members of this firm were architects who had won the Pritzker prize, acknowledged worldwide as a high honour in the architectural profession.

Despite these efforts, however, the national park authority remained opposed. Dr. Leeson adamantly opposed the location and design of this structure and insisted that it be relocated to a less intrusive position where it could be screened by trees that might also protect the structure from avalanches. The President of Canadian Pacific Limited, W.L. Stinson came to the hearing because of the extreme importance of the project to the company and he watched as the railway's lawyers cross-examined Dr. Leeson with great vigour.

As in all cases where legal counsel represents one party and the other party is not represented the park officials were caught off guard by the pressure of the railway's cross-examination, and they probably felt disadvantaged in the public hearing forum. They were still nursing their wounds on the following day when the Commission reconvened to hear the final argument. Canadian Pacific made a strong case for the necessity of the tunnel project for the good of the country and for the efficient operations of Canadian Pacific. The national parks officials maintained their general opposition from the previous day.

The mood of the parks officials was not improved by the fact that, immediately after Mr. Mullins rested his case, a written interim decision approving the tunnel project was delivered from the bench by the Commission. But the Pacific Railway had always been the historic backbone of Canadian efforts at transcontinental nation-building and the Rodgers Pass tunnel case was the last significant milestone toward the full utilization of the transcontinental railway as a national line of communication.

In its interim decision, the Commission granted the railway permission to build the tunnel project but made it clear that it would impose substantial environmental protection conditions in its final decision. The final decision of the Commission, issued in March 1982, went further by noting the splendour of Glacier National Park and calling for a dialogue between the railway company and the national parks authority. The Commission noted that both had resided in proximity to each other for about a century without serious differences and it called on both parties to cooperate in the completion of the tunnel project in an acceptable manner. Turning to the ventilation shaft issue, the Commission directed that alternate sites should be explored that would be less environmentally intrusive. The Commission created a working group from amongst its technical staff to monitor construction activities and to ensure compliance with all environmental protection measures mandated by the Commission.

A string of construction railcars loaded with muck excavated from the Mount Macdonald tunnel (photo: JC Cant)

Parks Canada officials were unhappy with the Commission's decision and now resorted to the use of their powers to address their continuing environmental concerns. Although the 1973 federal environmental assessment and review process was an administrative mechanism, it contained a provision that allowed the federal government to establish an environmental review panel to assess the environmental consequences of a proposed project, and to make appropriate recommendations concerning the mitigation of adverse environmental effects of a particular project if it was to proceed.

The national park authority now persuaded its Minister, the Hon. John Roberts PC, MP, that an environmental assessment review panel should be created to assess the tunnel project. An environmental assessment review panel was formed and it proceeded to conduct an environmental review in a deliberate manner. The presence of lawyers was discouraged and the review was not conducted along quasi-judicial lines. Several significant improvements were made to the environmental protection of the project as a result of the formal environmental review. In particular, the ventilation shaft and its massive head-house were relocated and redesigned to be far less intrusive. That change was costly to Canadian Pacific since the shaft had now to be sunk through overburden, rather than sunk into rock and compact soil. The overburden (which some of our engineers described as "loon-shit") was very loose and presented significant engineering challenges in the construction of the shaft. But the greatest cost to the railway company was in time, as the environmental review added eighteen months to the projected timeline for project completion. It was a clear indication of the growing importance of environmental issues in a public regulatory law practice.

The massive headhouse (shown under construction) was relocated to a less intrusive position within Glacier National Park (photo: JC Cant)

But nothing could take away from Canadian Pacific worthy praise for the sheer marvel of the tunnel project as a technical achievement. The project encompassed two tunnels for a total length exceeding ten miles, as well as five new bridges and a 4020-foot viaduct, in addition to other surface trackage. The Mt. Macdonald tunnel, appropriately named after the nation's first Prime Minister, whose legacy to the country was the transcontinental railway, was constructed in a horseshoe shape from both ends. At one end the Manning-Kumagai Joint Venture bore through the mountain in an easterly direction with a conventional blast and drill method while Selkirk Tunnel Contractors bored westward with a mole, which is a circular boring machine that cut a hole twenty-two feet wide in the mountain. The contractors used global satellite positioning and laser beams to bring the two ends together deep under the mountains.

With the completion of the Rodgers Pass tunnel project in the mid-eighties, the final operating challenges to efficient railway operations presented by the Rocky Mountains were swept away and the great policy dream of nineteenth century statesmen which called for an effective and efficient transcontinental railway link between eastern and western Canada was fully realized.

PART II.

RAIL LINE RATIONALIZATION

CHAPTER 3.

THE LAST WHISTLE

Across the western provinces and territories stretched a vast network of branch lines of railways that collected commodities for transportation to the ports on the Great Lakes, Hudson Bay, or the Pacific for export from Canada, or transportation to other land destinations within Canada. In the expansionist railway phase of western Canada in the late nineteenth and early twentieth centuries there had been a proliferation of main and branch line systems constructed to bring in settlers and the manufactured goods they required, and carrying out of the west all of the grain and other commodities that they newly settled west produced. On each line, the railways established stations approximately six miles apart, since a round trip of twelve miles by horse and cart was considered optimal. Although not all of the stations succeeded in attracting a permanent settlement, many flourished by attracting settlers who eventually spread across the wide expanse of the Prairie.

The impulse to construct an extensive main and branch line network was based on the soundest economic forecasting of the day. However, nineteenth-century railway optimism could not but fail to account for many variables, notably the future revolution in transportation that occurred with the invention and production of the internal combustion engine. As a result, the railway-based grain handling and distribution network was substantially overbuilt during the late nineteenth and early twentieth centuries.

Although the overbuilt rail network initially had no substantial negative economic impact on the railways, over time the collapse in western immigration, the effects of the Great Depression, the restrictions on revenue generation posed by the Crow Rate, the competition for the transport of high-value goods posed by trucks and finally postwar inflation all combined to undermine the economic position of the railways in respect of their grain networks. The cash drain could have proved fatal if the federal government had not stepped in to support the system in the sixties by instituting a statutory subsidy program under the *Railway Act*[1] to compensate the railways for the losses they incurred by continuing to operate an unprofitable grain gathering system.

Once the public treasury became responsible for funding the uneconomic branch line program railway subsidies became one of the government's largest continuing industrial transfer programs, creating a financial impetus to pare back the system to economic proportions. Of course, that created a potential for a public backlash and it was certainly true that no Western politician could speak frankly about abandoning Western railway branch lines without risking the wrath of the electorate. Nonetheless, several abandonments did occur during the seventies, often without a public hearing, which only fueled Western antipathies to branch-line abandonments.

The political solution was the tried and true method of placing the problem into the hands of a commission. The federal government established the Grain Handling and Transportation Commission and appointed the Honourable Emmett Hall, formerly a Justice of the Supreme Court of Canada, to preside over it. Emmett Hall proved to be an excellent choice. He was a Saskatchewan native and a Diefenbaker appointee to the Supreme Court who had now retired to Saskatoon, where he was well-remembered as a key person in the creation of state-funded healthcare, due to his landmark inquiry in the sixties into med-

---

1. *Railway Act*, RSC 1985, c. R-2

ical care in Saskatchewan. He was generally well-regarded by those on both the right and the left of the political spectrum in the West.

The Hall Commission began its work in April 1975 and investigated the disposition of 6,283 miles of grain-handling lines in western Canada. Before the Hall Commission, the federal cabinet had exercised its authority under the *Railway Act* to issue *Prohibition Orders* covering the entire western rail network. *Prohibition Orders* prevented the railways from seeking to abandon any line of a railway described in an order. Mr. Hall's task was to design an economically feasible basic rail network that would support the movement of western grain to export positions and allow many of the lines that would no longer be needed to be taken out of the protected network and referred to the CTC for an adjudication of their fate.

In April 1977, after the holding of an extensive series of public hearings in the West, the Hall Commission delivered its final report to the government. Approximately 1800 miles of trackage were recommended for inclusion in the grain-related rail network to be protected until the year 2000, and 2165 miles of trackage were recommended to be referred to the CTC for adjudication. The remainder was to be left to a new Prairie Rail Authority to determine its future status. The government accepted Mr. Hall's recommended additions to the Basic Rail Network to be protected until the year 2000.

Although the Hall Commission Report was favourably received in general, it was only to be expected that those who resided near lines that were not protected would be disappointed. Responding to their concerns, the government appointed a Prairie Rail Action Committee (PRAC) to review the lines which the Hall Commission had recommended be referred to a new Prairie Rail Authority. The PRAC reviewed approximately 2344 miles of trackage and in its 1978 report the PRAC recommended that some 1044 miles of additional trackage should also be added to the basic rail network and the remainder be referred to the CTC for adjudication.

At that point, the general election of 1979 resulted in a change of government, and the incoming Clark Ministry appointed Mr. Doug Neil, a Progressive-Conservative MP from Swift Current, to conduct yet another review, this time of both the recommendations of the Hall Commission and the PRAC. His 1979 report looked at approximately 2900 miles of trackage and it resulted in a few hundred miles of additional trackage being protected from potential abandonment.

To a large extent then, only the least economically feasible lines were left for the CTC to consider. Nevertheless, the people who depended on those branch lines felt the potential loss of them keenly and the government braced itself for difficult political fallout. By creating the CTC Western Division in 1979, the government hoped that a Western-based adjudicator would militate against the adverse political effects of the abandonment process. While the economic costs of abandonment were superable, the social costs animated most of the inhabitants of communities located on threatened rail lines.

Many producers feared that without the railway branch line, their small towns and hamlets scattered across the Prairie would diminish or fail. For many rural Prairie residents, the gathering momentum of a clear trend toward urbanization in the rural west was difficult to accept. Already some communities had become ghost towns and it was inevitable that many others would follow. For those who had lived their lives in these communities, and who could remember their vibrancy and vitality as recently as the years immediately following World War II, it was a bleak prospect to contemplate.

Western producers on branch lines not forming part of the basic rail network waited to hear the fate of their lines following adjudication by the CTC Western Division. From the outset, the CTC Western Division took the view that it was vital to hold public hearings on branch lines where there was an operating elevator to ensure that the railway and everyone affected by abandonment would have a fair chance to explain the impacts of a potential abandonment on their particular circumstances. There needed to be as much transparency as possible, to contribute to a broader understanding, if not a broader consensus.

By 1981, when my participation in this process began, the CTC Western Division was already well underway with this process. Although we were poised to pursue a full docket of abandonment cases in the winter and spring of 1982, our plans were soon overshadowed by the government's announcement of pending changes to the Crow Rate, the established fixed freight rate for the carriage of grain by the railway companies. Because the issue of freight rates was so closely tied to the economic feasibility of the grain gathering and transportation system, the Provinces of Saskatchewan and Alberta brought motions before the Commission seeking relief from the prospect of further abandonments in the following terms:

> That the Commission strike all hearings from its spring docket and reschedule them at a later date in consideration of the Crow rate negotiations and the fact that a determination cannot be made as to whether a branch line is likely to continue to be uneconomic within the meaning of the *Railway Act*.
>
> That the Commission defer all decisions pending on applications to abandon grain-dependent branch lines; and
>
> That the Commission rescind its decision respecting the Canadian National Railways' Endiang Subdivision, which had been rendered after the Minster of Transport had made his announcement about forthcoming changes to the Crow rate.

These motions came on for hearing at the commencement of the abandonment hearing for Canadian National's Cudworth Subdivision at the courthouse in Prince Albert, Saskatchewan, on March 9, 1982. Prince Albert was in the heart of the prairie culture that had grown up alongside the grain economy. John Diefenbaker, a prairie political populist, had cut his teeth as a barrister in these same courtrooms where the Commission now sat before embarking on a political career that would take him to Ottawa, and the office of Prime Minister.

The courthouse in Prince Albert, Saskatchewan

The federal government's political decision to move away from the historic 1897 Crow Rate had changed the landscape of the branch-line abandonment debate, and it was clear that any attempt by the Commission to pursue branch-line abandonment while the 1897 rates were being dismantled could have sparked widespread discontent in the west. After due consideration, the motion brought by the two provinces was granted, at least concerning the request that all pending abandonment applications (including the Cudworth Subdivision) be delayed indefinitely. However, the Western Division Commissioners decided that they could not refuse to release judgments in abandonment cases that had been heard and reserved because the composition of the hearing panels differed in some cases from the composition of the panel that had heard the motions. That matter was therefore left to the individual hearing panels to deal with. Finally, the Province of Alberta was told that it must take its request for relief in respect of the Endiang decision to the CTC's Review Committee in Hull, Quebec, as the hearing panel had already exhausted all of its legal powers concerning that case once its decision on the abandonment application had been publicly issued.

Matters rested there through the spring and summer, giving Dr. Gilson, the government's grain freight rate facilitator, a decent interval to engage in consultations with stakeholders, and for the population to process the forthcoming changes and to prepare for them. Dr. Gilson's report was released on June 28, 1982, and it contained a recommendation to the CTC that the Commission should resume its series of branch line abandonment hearings. In the waning days of summer, the CTC Western Division therefore decided to proceed with an autumn abandonment hearing schedule and it wrote to the railway solicitors, as well as the solicitors for the provinces, on August 23, 1982, advising them that the pending hearings of abandonment applications would be recommenced.

A determined effort was made in late 1982 to schedule all of the outstanding applications to complete the initial adjudication of all abandonment cases left for the Commission by the various inquiries of the seventies. However, the province of Saskatchewan was not so easily persuaded of the need to continue with branch-line abandonment adjudications and it brought a new motion before the Commission to suspend all abandonment cases until Parliament had an opportunity to debate and enact the new western grain rate legislation that the government had promised. That motion was heard orally by the CTC Western Division on October 5 and 6, 1982.

This time the Commission was not persuaded that branch line abandonment applications should be deferred. After reserving judgement on the motion the CTC Western Division issued a ruling on October 13, 1982 (Decision WDR1982-12) which denied the Saskatchewan request. The CTC Western Division based its refusal for a further deferral of the abandonment cases on a 1949 judgement of the Supreme Court of Canada in similar circumstances involving the Commission's predecessor body, the Board of Transport Commissioners for Canada. In that case, the Supreme Court had said:

> ... it was not competent to the Board to await the investigation of such matters by some other body or the passing by Parliament of some future legislation with respect to them. Such a decision involves, in our opinion, a declining of jurisdiction[2].

The refusal to defer was issued while the CTC Western Division was on the road hearing abandonment cases. Saskatchewan was not pleased and as I sat one evening in a restaurant in a small Saskatchewan town listening to the televised news the newscaster reported that Saskatchewan Attorney General Gary Lane had asked for an opinion from the Province's counsel on the validity of the ruling. However, the ruling was sustainable as a matter of law and no further action was taken by the province, although rumblings of discontent from the Government of Saskatchewan continued throughout the autumn hearings.

The ambitious hearing schedule for the autumn of 1982 found the CTC Western Division in Saskatchewan, at Hudson Bay on September 16 for a hearing on the CN Erwood Subdivision, in Prince Albert on September 29 for the hearing on the CN Cud-

---

2. *Canadian Pacific Railway v Province of Alberta et al*, [1950] SCR 25 (SCC)

worth Subdivision, in Moose Jaw for hearings into the CN Central Butte Subdivision on October fifth, and in Avonlea on the sixth for the CN Avonlea Subdivision hearing, then to Canora on the October 13 for a hearing about the CN Rhein Subdivision and in Weekes on October 14 to hear the CN Chelan Subdivision abandonment case. Next, the CTC Western Division ventured east into Manitoba, to Fork River on October 19 to hold a hearing concerning the CN Winnipegosis Subdivision and then to Fisher Branch on October 21 for a hearing about the CN Inwood Subdivision. After a brief interval, the Commission traveled into Alberta to hear the CN Bodo Subdivision case on November 16 and returned to Saskatchewan to hear the CN Preeceville Subdivision on November 18, the CP Colony Subdivision on November 23 and the CP Fife Lake Subdivision on November 24, ending with the CP Pennant Subdivision on the 30th of November.

All abandonment cases followed a general pattern of informality, although each displayed its unique characteristics. Before the hearing, the Commission would issue a Notice of Hearing, and a Determination of Actual Loss for the accounting years prescribed by regulation (i.e., the prior three years). A public report with a map of the line under review containing pertinent information for hearing participants was prepared and distributed at the hearing. The information contained in the booklet included the Notice, an application history, the history of the line, a description of the physical condition of the line, operational data, a statement of actual losses, traffic data, elevator storage capacity, grain delivery data, the closest alternative delivery points, the population figures for points along the line, a synopsis of the Hall, PRAC, and Neil studies, a copy of the pertinent part of the railway operating timetable, a description of the grain block shipping system[3], and a map of the area.

---

3. See the Appendix for a description of the grain car allocation system.

Usually, we traveled to the hearing location by car, although occasionally we chartered a Beechcraft King Air from Hi-Line, a local charter air service in Saskatoon, and flew to an unmanned airstrip near the hearing location. In most cases the hearing was held in a local community hall, often somewhat tattered by the passing of the years and sometimes equipped with a mounted deer or elk head, or a faded portrait of the Monarch mounted upon a wall. Two or three tables would be set up at the front on a raised dais facing the rest of the room to serve as a bench for the commissioners. The tables were dressed with white tablecloth skirts that extended to the floor. Looking upwards towards the bench from the places reserved for that audience, the left front table would be appropriated by the Commission counsel and the staff of the Commission while possession of the right front table was taken by the railway counsel and his or her advisors. To the far right, adjacent to the bench and the table for the railway counsel, a table was set up for witnesses that was positioned at a ninety-degree angle to the bench. Witnesses were allowed to take the stand in groups as a single panel if a party desired. A small table was set up in front and below the commissioners (or to one side) for the court reporters, and Louise Cyr, our Hearing Process Officer (essentially our court clerk), occupied a small desk to the left of the commission counsel that was situated on a 45-degree angle so that her eye could be caught by either the commissioners or legal counsel. Somewhere in the building, there was usually a kitchen facility and while the hearing continued local women would often prepare a luncheon for all of the participants. Lunch was served cafeteria style and everyone ate at their seats during a one-hour lunch break.

Abandonment hearings were always significant social and political events in a small community and a normal abandonment hearing could bring out two or three hundred people, including all of the local political notables. Signs were erected to direct participants to the proper location. Although the signs typically referred to the rail abandonment hearing, I was struck by the optimism I encountered at Weekes, Saskatchewan, on the CN Chelan Subdivision, where the signs referred to the rail <u>retention</u> hearing rather than to a rail <u>abandonment</u> hearing. The power of positive thinking should not be underestimated, as the Chelan Subdivision was ordered to be retained following the 1982 hearing.

As the Commission was a court of record, everyone was asked to rise by the Hearing Process Officer as she announced the entry of the members of the Commission. That, and Commissioner Bernie Wolfe's insistence that all men doff their caps, were the main formalities. Hearings involving the Canadian National Railway Company tended to be more relaxed than Canadian Pacific hearings. Canadian National's Winnipeg-based regional counsel, Grant Nerbas used a non-confrontational approach in his handling of the objections to abandonment. Although the lawyers for Canadian Pacific also recognized the political dimension to these hearings, they represented one of the major corporations in the country, and one that had at various times in the past sparked particular resentment among rural Westerners. They were very businesslike in their dealings with the public and with the Commission and perhaps they recalled a famous statement attributed to one of the company's chief executives, Ian Sinclair, who was reputed to have said that at Canadian Pacific "all litigation was a tool of business".

After the calling of formal appearances by the Hearing Process Officer (from everyone who had filled out a registration form) and the introduction into evidence of the most recent (preliminary) loss figures by me, the railway counsel would call the witnesses for the railways who would be sworn, or affirmed, by the Hearing Process Officer. Railway counsel would then lead them through their direct evidence which was generally contained in a prepared written document.

After examination in chief by the railway counsel, I would cross-examine the railway witnesses on their evidence. This was a variation of the normal hearing procedure under which registered interveners would normally proceed before Commission counsel asked any questions on behalf of the Commission. In the case of abandonment files the local participants had a natural reserve since public hearings were an unfamiliar forum to most and it was considered to be desirable to let the Commission counsel identify any weaknesses in the railway's case before local interveners were invited to ask questions. It also gave the participants an example to follow when they came forward to question the railway's witnesses.

After I finished asking questions, generally taking 30 to 60 minutes, the floor was opened to the other participants (basically, anyone present who wished to question the railway was given legal standing as an intervener) to ask questions of the railway witnesses. After all of the interveners had been allowed to ask questions the Commissioners might ask a few questions and the railway would reexamine its witnesses concerning any new matters that had arisen in the course of the cross-examination of the railway witnesses.

Evidence was then presented by interveners, either individually or as part of a group, and their evidence was likewise subject to cross-examination by the railway counsel, other interveners if they did not support the interveners who were testifying, and then finally by me. Afterwards, the Commissioners might ask a few questions if they wished. Before any local interveners were called upon the Commission would invite the local political representatives who were present to testify.

For a Federal Member of Parliament, even a cabinet minister, it was essential to be seen at a CTC abandonment hearing occurring in their riding and to be seen fighting to save the local branch line. So invariable was this rule that when the veteran

Alvin Hamilton, a sitting M.P. and a Diefenbaker era cabinet minister, failed to show up at the abandonment hearing in respect of the CP Corning Subdivision in 1986, I knew immediately that it meant he would not stand again at a general election. Members of the Legislative Assembly of a Province, including cabinet ministers, also attended abandonment hearings to fight for the retention of their local line even though rail policy was an area of federal jurisdiction. The participation of the local political leadership often added colour to the proceedings

The provinces officially participated through representatives from the provincial departments of transportation. Politically, it was an easy call for the provinces to ask the Commission to retain particular branch lines since rail policy was a federal issue, and the provinces knew that none of the financial consequences of retention would accrue to them, or to the companies under their jurisdiction.

Elevator companies with facilities on the line also participated in the proceedings. Some of the public or private corporations operating elevators would be forthcoming in stating their corporate plans to phase out operations at a particular location. However, the producer-owned pools that operated elevators in each province, Manitoba Pool, Saskatchewan Wheat Pool, and Alberta Wheat Pool, found themselves in an unenviable position. As cooperative associations rather than true corporations their internal politics prevented them from actually stating that they would phase out operations at elevator stations located on those grain-dependent branch lines that were not part of the basic rail network. Instead, they offered set-piece advice to the Commission, pledging to upgrade their elevators if the line was retained and rehabilitated.

The elevator companies thus hid their true intentions and publicly opposed abandonments although privately accepting it as a necessary means to rationalize the overextended rail and elevator networks in the west. The elevator companies were beginning to plan for a system of new high-throughput elevators and inland terminals. These facilities were many times more efficient than the old wooden sentinels of the prairies, the country elevators. Additionally, unlike the antiquated country elevator system, inland terminals permitted the cleaning of grain on the Prairie and the screenings available from the cleaning process could be quickly reintegrated into Prairie agriculture through feedlots. Cleaning grain on the Prairies also relieved congestion at the port terminals, which enhanced the overall efficiency of the grain handling and transportation system.

Branch line abandonment hearings attracted two groups; those who had a good knowledge of the overall policy objectives of branch line rationalization such as governments, federal and provincial politicians, railways, and elevator companies, and secondly producers, local governments, and residents, who viewed the issues through the prism of local impacts. Most of the local inhabitants felt that the loss of the railway and the local country elevator would reduce the number of people coming into town with a consequent loss to local businesses. Local commerce would decline and the community would begin a downward economic spiral. Ultimately, the community could fail and a way of life in the small Prairie grain communities would disappear.

Such views were keenly felt by many of the ordinary people of Manitoba, Saskatchewan, and Alberta with whom I came into contact during this period. It was not uncommon to see multiple generations in a single-family appear at a hearing and present a united front in opposition to the loss of the local rail line. On one occasion, I recall seeing four generations from within a single family take the witness stand to plead for the retention of their local branch line.

The real issue for these communities was not the immediate transportation problem, although that was an important factor, but the societal process of urbanization which was occurring regardless of the presence of a railway line in a particular rural community. Saskatchewan provided a good example of this process. In the immediate aftermath of World War One Saskatchewan possessed the third highest population among Canadian provinces with approximately one million residents, a position which reflected the Province's strong rural base. As the years passed, Saskatchewan was surpassed in population by other provinces which attracted residents to their cities. Although the urbanization process affected Saskatchewan too, the growth in Saskatchewan was slower owing to the absence of a large industrial base in the province that was attractive to migrants. Nevertheless, by 1966 Saskatchewan had crossed the urbanization threshold with more than 50% of its population now residing in urban areas.

The longer and slower pace of urbanization across the Prairie gave hope to those who thought that urbanization trends could be forestalled from shrinking many small villages and hamlets into oblivion. The local rail line was seen as a key ingredient in maintaining local economic vitality, and of the rural society that had been established on the foundation of the grain economy.

It was important for the CTC Western Division to remain sensitive to these attitudes and concerns among the residents of communities faced with the loss of their local branch line. In an ever faster-paced society, it was particularly important to remember that not everyone participated in societal transience. As the average age in small towns increased a palpable sense of loss arose with urbanization taking younger people away to the cities.

Nevertheless, for many of the small communities faced with branch line abandonment, the economic die had already been cast. The town of Weekes in eastern Saskatchewan, located on the CN Chelan Subdivision, was a case in point. The statistical information available to the Commission at the time of its 1982 hearing showed that the community had suffered a loss of 80% of its population since the end of World War Two.

As counsel, I did appreciate the opportunity presented by these hearings to deal with real people and their aspirations for their communities. The ingenuity of the arguments presented by interveners seeking to save their threatened rail line was remarkable. Often the case for retention took the form of identifying some other commodity that could be hauled away by the railway at a profit. Thus it was suggested that threatened rail lines would be needed for the exploitation of sodium sulphate (CP Pennant Subdivision; Decision WDR1982-18, pg.7), limestone (CN Winnipegosis Subdivision; Decision WDR1983-02, pg 7), dolomite, marble, Kaolin clay, gravel and lumber (CN Inwood Subdivision; Decision WDR1983-03, pg. 9) coal and clay (CP Fife Lake Subdivision; Decision WDR1983-05, pg.7), helium (CP Colony Subdivision Decision WDR1982-15), and bentonite (CN Avonlea Subdivision; Decision WDR1983-15, pg.7). Virtually all opponents of branch line abandonment argued that the local rail line could handle a much larger amount of grain.

One economic response of the railways to the fixed rate structure was to defer maintenance on grain-dependent branch lines. That policy worked for a while but the sheer length of time that the unrevised Crow Rate existed eventually led to a serious decline in the efficiency and safety of the branch line network. Balanced against whatever potential there was for increased grain production or the exploitation of some hitherto overlooked resource was the cost of rehabilitating the rail line to a standard that would be acceptable for the transport of modern carloads. The government responded by creating a rehabilitation program. During this period the federal government began bankrolling the Prairie Branch Line Rehabilitation Program at a cost of nine hundred million dollars to make up for the lack of required maintenance during the period since the Crow Rate had been established in 1897.

Travelling to the site of a branch line rehabilitation project by Hi-Rail vehicles

The rehab program (as it was called) standard required a track structure that could support year-round operations of trains capable of carrying cars with a gross weight of 220,000 tonnes (later revised to 263,000 tonnes) at 30 miles per hour. Many of the lines under review by the CTC were in such poor condition that the cost of restoring and upgrading them would have proved prohibitive[4]. The CTC Western Division administered the tech-

---

4. It was not only a question of repairing the track structure. The branch line network had been originally constructed with 60-pound or 80-pound rail which had become outdated. As a result, the railway companies were unable to load modern hopper cars fully or to use their modern locomotives on the old branch line network. The CN maintained a roster of specially-built light locomotives (GMD 1000 series engines) for working its western branch line network. Sometimes switching locomotives were also used on the light rail branch lines. The CP was also restricted to lighter railcars and locomotives on its outdated branch line network. The rehab program involved a significant upgrading of the track structure to include at least 100-pound rail to accommodate the heavier equipment.

nical side of the rehab program on behalf of the Department of Transport. This responsibility also gave the Western Division an entrée into the policy side of the program. Essentially, this was a central planning process with the government and the railways selecting the lines that would become eligible for rehab funds. The CTC Western Division retained a technical consultant (initially Bill Cumine later succeeded by René Lessard) to assist our engineering director with this work.

Officials gather for a last spike ceremony on the new CN Imperial Subdivision, built as a connection and transfer between the CN Watrous Subdivision and the CP Amazon Subdivision

Hammering home the last spike

Nevertheless, despite the central planning exercise a few lines reserved for the consideration of the CTC did make it into the program on the CTC Western Division's recommendation following abandonment hearings, which was the goal of every opponent of branch line abandonment during the eighties. For example, the CN Carleton Subdivision was retained and put into the rehabilitation program even though the infrastructure was in such poor condition that it was commonly made subject to out-of-service orders in the summer due to sun kinks, resulting from the heat of the Prairie sun causing the century-old rail to buckle!

In some instances where it was still viable to retain some portion of a branch line the rehab program paid for the construction of a connection line between the two mainline railways to facilitate the transfer of a portion of a branch line from CP to CN or vice versa. Such transfers allowed the remaining trackage of the transferor railway to be abandoned while the transferee railway maintained service to a still viable grain delivery point.

Other lines were retained for indefinite periods without necessarily obtaining entry to the rehabilitation program. The CN Erwood and Chelan Subdivisions were retained to handle bridge traffic. The CP Colony line was kept because of the potential for new resources to develop. Occasionally, there were brief reprieves, such as a decision in respect of the CN Amiens Subdivision which ordered that the line be abandoned unless it could reach a particular elevator throughput objective. The abandonment of the CP Wishart Subdivision was briefly delayed when the CTC Western Division discovered that the line was actually owned by the Manitoba and Northwestern Railway Company, a defunct but not extinguished Canadian Pacific subsidiary that had given its parent a long-term lease of the line. To ensure that the abandonment application was legal, Canadian Pacific was required by the CTC Western Division to resuscitate its moribund subsidiary by appointing a Board of Directors, locating the corporate seal, and then convening a meeting of the Board of Directors to pass a resolution to endorse the parent company's abandonment application. Only after all the technical legal requirements were met was the abandonment allowed to proceed.

Given the uneconomic nature of the lines under review, it was only to be expected that most of the lines would be ordered abandoned, although, for the communities located along the few lines that were given a reprieve, there was undoubtedly an increase in local morale and spirit. On one occasion when I was attending to some business at the Courthouse in Winnipeg, I fell into conversation with a Court of Queen's Bench Justice who told me that when he was still in practice in rural Manitoba no case had given him greater satisfaction than his defense of his community's local branch line before the Board of Transport Commissioners. He still recalled the triumph of sitting in his car some months after the hearing when the radio announcer stated that the Board had ordered the line to be continued in service. But such reprieves were not the norms, and more often than not they were only temporary when they did occur. When I asked the Manitoba Justice whether his community's branch line still existed he shook his head sadly and said no.

In British Columbia, there was a less extensive branch line network than that which existed on the Prairies, and the same public pressures did not exist in our westernmost province when it came to abandonment cases. In British Columbia, the railway had lost much of its day-to-day importance to local inhabitants and it remained primarily of use to the resource industries of coal, lumber, and pulp and paper. Some minor abandonments of lines on Vancouver Island occurred during the eighties but our most significant case in the province involved the abandonment of the Canadian Pacific Kaslo Subdivision, lying deep in the Kootenay Mountains. Despite the high costs of operating the line and its associated rail car ferry across Slocan Lake, the CTC Western Division was persuaded by the lumber interests that transportation alternatives were limited, owing to the treacherous mountain roads, which in one place reduced motor vehicles to a single lane of traffic, and by the problems expressed with long loads of poles grounding on the highway ferry apron at Galena Bay. The line was ordered to be retained.

British Columbia was also the setting for the abandonment of the line that I thought was in the worst physical condition. The line in question was Burlington Northern's 8th Subdivision extension from Chopaka Washington to Keremeos, B.C. In Decision WDR1985-07, the Commission found that (p.2):

A survey of the line disclosed that weeds and trees have grown over the track ties and rails, shoulders of the grade have been eroded and some sections of the track have been removed. A number of the long bridges have been washed away by floods. In some areas, the ties and rails have sunk into the grade and become covered with mud. Cawston station, at mile 156.90 is in extremely poor condition and is subject to vandalism.

Needless to say, there was no longer a public need for this line and the Commission authorized its abandonment.

Even though the fate of many rail lines was virtually a foregone conclusion based on the actual losses which they were incurring residents faced with the prospect of losing their rail line were not without a legal remedy. Applications could be made to the CTC's Review Committee in Hull, Quebec, seeking to overturn abandonment orders because new facts had arisen, circumstances had changed, or that the Commission had exceeded its jurisdiction, or erred in law. Generally, those applications were unsuccessful although, in a few instances, they led to a further consideration of the effects of the abandonment on services that would continue to be offered by the railways on the trackage to be retained, or an extension of the effective date of the abandonment order as a transitional measure.

Appeals could also be lodged with the Federal Court of Appeal, with leave of that court, claiming that the Commission had exceeded its jurisdiction or erred in law. Few attempts to appeal western abandonment orders succeeded in reaching an appeal hearing. One that did, and which caused some trouble from a subsidy administration perspective, concerned a peculiar joint Canadian National and Canadian Pacific section of trackage between Rosedale and East Coulee in Alberta. This small section of trackage was constructed in the twenties by both railways to avoid costly competition between them for the local coal traffic that originated near Drumheller, Alberta. By the eighties, the slumping demand for coal had rendered the railway line uneconomic and the railways sought permission to abandon it. While coal was no longer taken from mines in the area one local coal company had surface stockpiles from its Atlas mine which it still hoped to sell, and therefore it objected to the abandonment. The Commission nevertheless granted an abandonment order and the coal company together with the city of Drumheller challenged that order on the grounds that a special Act of Parliament enacted in the twenties prevailed over the *Railway Act,* and that the special Act required that the line be operated in perpetuity. In a split decision, the Federal Court of Appeal overturned the abandonment order on the ground that the special Act applied and that it required perpetual operation of the line[5].

The railways sought leave to appeal the Federal Court decision to the Supreme Court of Canada and it was the practice in those days for the Supreme Court to hold oral hearings for leave to appeal applications. I appeared on behalf of the Commission at the oral hearing of the leave application, which was granted[6].

5. When I appeared before the Federal Court of Appeal for the first time on behalf of the Commission at the hearing of this appeal in Edmonton in the autumn of 1982 I admit to being a little intimidated by the fact that Chief Justice Thurlow, who presided at the appeal, had at that time been on the Federal Court and its predecessors longer than I had been alive!

6. The panel consisted of Justice Roland Ritchie as President of the panel with Justices McIntyre and Estey. Justice Ritchie waited until after the court had heard from all of the counsel for the parties before calling on me very affably and stating: "We haven't forgotten about you Mr. Noonan" and asked me for my representations. Justice Estey quickly interjected with "Mr. Noonan you are restricted to submissions on the question of jurisdiction" which was a firm reminder of my duties as a friend of the court and an injunction which I was quick to acknowledge. My representations substantively focussed on the jurisdiction of the Commission and how the Federal Court of Appeal's divided judgement had raised a question of the Commission's jurisdiction upon which it was desirable to obtain legal certainty. That prompted the court to ask me several questions about how the Federal Court of Appeal's judgement could impact the work of the Commission in other cases. The legal questions that were raised by that case had arisen in at least two other cases that awaited resolution and I was able to explain those circumstances to the court. The panel eventually granted leave to appeal. Ultimately, I appeared at the hearing of the appeal essentially as an *amicus curiae* on behalf of the Commission.

In the meantime however, the coal company ceased to do business and dropped out of the proceedings[7]. The City likewise ceased to take an interest in the proceeding. Railway counsel then attempted to have the judgement of the Federal Court of Appeal overturned by consent of all the parties. This proved impossible however when the *rota* judge in the Supreme Court of Canada, Madam Justice Bertha Wilson, refused to allow a judgement of the Federal Court of Appeal based on statutory jurisdiction to be overturned on consent without a hearing.

At that point, the railways appeared to lose interest in the case. The CTC Western Division did not lose interest, however, as the federal treasury continued to pay subsidy charges for the line. After the passage of two years without any movement, the Commission directed one of its Inspecting Engineers, J.C. Cant, to examine the trackage and report back to the Commission. That report disclosed that the joint line had ceased to exist due to a lack of maintenance. At one point, a rockslide had buried the line. Despite its impassable status the line continued to attract public subsidies because, by law, it was still regarded as an operating branch line. The CTC Western Division issued an order suspending operations on the line and thereafter sought to suspend the subsidy payment based on the suspension of operations. The railways attacked that action in the Federal Court of Appeal and the Court granted leave to the railways to appeal the Commission's decision, with the judges in oral questioning seeming to suggest that the Commission's approach was dubious in law.

Nevertheless, all of this activity did finally prompt the railways to proceed with the outstanding appeal of the abandonment order

---

7. The company was the last coal producer in the area and although it had ceased to mine coal by 1980, it maintained surface stockpiles for some years into the eighties. Unfortunately, the type of coal it mined was not suitable for metallurgical uses and there were more economic sources of thermal coal. The mine was subsequently opened to public tours as a historical museum.

to the Supreme Court, and, in the summer of 1988, the matter came on for hearing before a five-judge bench of the Supreme Court of Canada. CP had overall carriage of the appeal and it was represented by their Calgary-based regional counsel, Marcella M. Szel, while Grant Nerbas appeared for the CN and I appeared for the Commission (now replaced by the National Transportation Agency). No one appeared for the City of Drumheller or Century Coals Ltd. When Mr. Nerbas was only a few minutes into his argument Chief Justice Dickson interrupted him to inquire why neither of the two Respondents, the City of Drumheller and the Century Coal Company, was present. Ms. Szel then intervened and stated that the respondents were no longer interested in the appeal. The Court then asked if the Commission had a different view than the railways and when apprised that it did not the Court decided to grant judgement on consent to overturn the judgement of the Federal Court of Appeal. The way was now cleared for the CTC's recent successor, the National Transportation Agency, to issue an abandonment order, which it thereafter proceeded to do and, in the summer of 1988, almost seven years after the original abandonment order had been issued, the branch line was finally ordered to be abandoned. The outstanding subsidy litigation was subsequently terminated by consent.

Apart from the remedies of administrative review or appeal which primarily had a legal focus, there was one other avenue of redress that opponents of branch line abandonments could avail themselves of. The *National Transportation Act* which governed the CTC gave the Governor General in Council (effectively the federal cabinet) the power to vary or rescind an abandonment order issued by the Commission. This was essentially a political remedy and opponents of abandonment decisions issued by the Commission hardly ever failed to take advantage of it by submitting a formal petition to the Crown.

Almost always petitions to the Governor in Council were denied but as the Privy Council office (which provided the administrative support to the Governor General in Council) was often unable to deal with a petition until the abandonment date was looming there was a danger that an abandonment order would take effect before the decision had been rendered. Notwithstanding the political nature of the remedy, it was considered essential by the CTC Western Division to stay the execution of its abandonment orders where a petition to the Governor in Council remained outstanding where an abandonment date loomed. That necessitated that I maintain close contact with one of the lawyers for the Privy Council, usually Jean Bellmare, to update the status of petitions filed with the Governor General in Council.

Unquestionably, emotions ran high in branch line abandonment cases – especially when the local inhabitants had exhausted almost all of the remedies available to them to prevent the abandonment. A good example of how the emotions could spill over into a crisis occurred in the late summer of 1982. An abandonment order was scheduled to take effect on the Asquith Subdivision near Saskatoon. The standard practice was to fix the abandonment date for August 31st. The rationale for using that date was that the annual Canadian Wheat Board crop year ended on July 31st of each year so an August 31st abandonment date would allow uninterrupted elevator and rail operations to continue until the end of a crop year. The elevator companies would then terminate their active operations at points on lines to be abandoned at the end of July, and the extra month after the end of the crop year allowed the Canadian Wheat Board and the railways to clean out the existing elevator stocks from the elevators in preparation for abandonment.

The abandonment order for the Asquith Subdivision was scheduled to take effect on August 31, 1982. However, a petition by the local rail retention committee was still before the Governor in Council. A request had been received from the Asquith Subdivision Rail Line Retention Committee for a stay of execution pending the decision of the Governor in Council and it was deemed necessary to preserve the rail line pending a final resolution of the branch line's status. Accordingly, a very short stay of execution of the abandonment order amounting to no more than a few days was granted. When the petition was subsequently denied no further extension of the abandonment order was warranted, and the abandonment order took effect early in September.

The denial of the petition led to an uproar in the community over the fact that the retentionists had lost their final appeal and that within a very short period their petition was denied, the stay of execution expired, and the branch line had been legally abandoned. The local grain producers decided to take matters into their own hands and they came together with their tractors and other farm vehicles and placed them on the rail line, thus blockading Canadian Pacific from removing the rails and other branch line facilities. The blockade became a local cause célèbre and it was widely reported upon in the local media. Canadian Pacific was forced to dispatch one of its Winnipeg-based lawyers to appear in the Court of Queen's Bench in Saskatoon and obtain an injunction against the Asquith area grain producers. Eventually, passions cooled and the railway was then able to send in its work crews to dismantle the branch line[8].

8. Coordination of the abandonment process was not only important in the context of grain-dependent branch lines. It was also important in the case of resource-dependent branch lines in BC. On one occasion when the CN was attempting to abandon branch lines on Vancouver Island, there were concerns that the railway might terminate its marine barge service between the mainland and the island, thus effectively abandoning the services on the island before all of the review applications were determined. The CTC Western Division was bound by a previous decision of the Federal Court of Appeal which found that a railway barge was not part of the railway for the purposes of branch line abandonments. However, the Commission's general jurisdiction over the activities of the corporation allowed it to issue a formal directive requiring the railway to provide 30 days advance notice before terminating barge services to ensure that shippers would at least have advance warning of any cessation of service.

The controversy surrounding the abandonment of the Asquith Subdivision was a lesson in the strong views and tenacity of the opponents of branch line abandonments. Sometimes the opponents would fight on to try to save a branch line even after the abandonment order had taken effect. In one singular case, the opponents were actually able to reverse a decision to abandon a branch line after an abandonment decision had gone into effect and to force a restoration of service.

Following a hearing in the autumn of 1982, the Commission ordered the CP Fife Lake Subdivision to be abandoned on August 31, 1984. The line was actually abandoned on that date but Canadian Pacific did not move quickly enough to take up the rails and other branch line facilities. A few days later a federal general election led to the replacement of the Liberal Ministry of John Turner with a Progressive Conservative Ministry headed by Brian Mulroney. A member of Parliament from southern Saskatchewan, Mr. Len Gustafson, was named Parliamentary Secretary to the Prime Minister and soon rumblings were heard by the CTC Western Division about the abandonment of the Fife Lake line, which lay in Mr. Gustafson's riding.

Under the *Railway Act*, no line of railway constructed by a railway company could legally bear traffic until the Commission had opened the line for the carriage of traffic. Ordinarily, such applications were made only by the railway company and were extinguished by an abandonment order. Mr. Gustafson now applied to the Commission for an order under an obscure provision of the *Railway Act,* section 217, that allowed persons other than a railway company to apply to open a railway for the carriage of traffic. Although an independent observer might have concluded that a reopening of the line could not be done in the face of an abandonment order it soon became clear that some kind of an arrangement had been made between Mr. Gustafson and the railway company, with the politics of the situation being an obvious and important factor for the railway company. In response to Mr. Gustafson's application, the Canadian Pacific filed a one-line letter opposing the use of section 217 of the *Railway Act* to restore the Fife Lake Subdivision. Faced with something of a dilemma, the CTC Western Division found a tenuous basis in law to support the restoration of the Fife Lake Subdivision. Nothing further was heard from Canadian Pacific about the matter and the CP Fife Lake Subdivision earned the distinction of becoming the only branch line that was legally abandoned and then restored to service[9].

In some instances, branch lines were abandoned by a company without a complete cessation of elevator services to adjacent grain-producing areas. In those cases the Hall Commission, or the Prairie Rail Action Committee, had recommended that connections be built between a grain delivery point and an adjacent line, such as, for example, between Fosston on the CP Tisdale Subdivision and Kelvington on the (to be) abandoned CN Preeceville Subdivision, or that a connection be built between two lines and that part of a line be abandoned and the part beyond the connection be retained or transferred if the connection was built to another railway. In such cases, the Commission exercised a review and coordination role through its abandonment powers. Sometimes the Commission had to be creative in finding ways to ensure that the public was accommodated and not disrupted in these circumstances. In one example (referred to in Decision WDR1985-09, pg 1) the Commission had to invoke rarely used emergency powers enacted by Parliament

---

9. In the year before I joined the CTC Western Division, the CP had sought and obtained permission to reopen part of the legally abandoned Miniota Subdivision for OCS (on company service) traffic, as the railway realized that it needed to haul ballast supplies from a quarry located on the abandoned line. The chairman of the local rail retention committee, who had been unsuccessful in his attempt to save the line for grain transport, was subsequently struck by a slow-moving train when he drove his tractor across what he thought was an abandoned branch line. The Commission ensured in subsequent similar situations that the railway company always gave public notice of any temporary resumption of rail operations on a legally abandoned branch line.

during a grain transportation crisis in World War I to ensure the movement of stocks of grain out of an elevator before a pending connection and transfer rendered further service to an elevator impossible.

Branch line connections formed part of the infrastructure funded by the government under the Prairie Branch Line Rehabilitation Program. The legal work associated with this program was mostly standard solicitors' work but in one instance we had to convene a special hearing. The Minister of Transport, with the concurrence of the Governor General in Council, appointed Commissioner McDonough as an Inquiry Officer under the *National Transportation Act* to examine the detailed route for a proposed new connecting branch line near Colonsay, Saskatchewan. Canadian National was responsible for building the connection to the existing CP Colonsay Subdivision, and thereafter accepting a transfer of the portion of the line to be saved from Canadian Pacific.

Canadian National examined three possible routes, and that fact became well known to the residents of the area who observed the railway surveyors in their fields. As is often the case when significant infrastructure projects are undertaken there was significant opposition from those persons whose lands would be required for the project. A great deal of opposition was voiced to the CN in the Colonsay case, as well as to political representatives concerning this connection project. The Minister wanted an Inquiry to determine which of the routes proposed by the CN was the most desirable, taking into account all perspectives. I served as counsel to this Inquiry.

The Inquiry requested that the railway locate and provide cost estimates for a hypothetical fourth route that was about two miles further west. That route proved to be economically unfeasible in the end (although it had a few interesting operational advantages) but it had the unfortunate effect of stirring up additional landowners in the area, who retained counsel to represent them at the Inquiry. In the end, the Inquiry selected a route that followed the surveyed section line and thus did the least damage to existing farmsteads, which quieted the opposition.

The difficulty posed by the rehab program was that it represented static planning undertaken in the seventies, and the decisions taken during the formative planning stages were increasingly overtaken by new events in the eighties, such as variable freight rates for grain. By the time the program was completed, it was no longer clear whether all of the rehabilitated lines would last long enough to recoup the investments made in them.

The abandonment program represented a difficult exercise for the federal government, running as it did headlong into the Western public's perspective of the railways as an industry that was imbued with a public purpose. Nevertheless, the emphasis on decision-making from within the affected region, coupled with a regulatory policy of holding public hearings in affected locations eased the transition toward a more economically efficient grain collection and distribution system.

During this period the western arm of the Commission also dealt with other aspects of the rationalization of the railway services provided to western Canadians. One of these programs involved the cessation of local service by agents in small communities, where the existence of the rail line itself was not threatened by the withdrawal of service. Historically, local agents had been stationed by the railways in communities to provide all of the services that railway customers required. The station agent was the focal point of contact with the railway company for the public and they would arrange for shipments of goods, issuance of passenger tickets, and, in the smaller communities, they provided, at one time, telegraph services using the old Morse code system.

While the agent's presence made sense when the railways had few transportation competitors, the role of agents was undermined by advances in new modes of transport. At one time a station agent was located in most of the communities served by a railway. As highways improved, more and more of the railway's high-value traffic went to the motor carriers. In the late sixties, CN closed its less-than-carload traffic department. Improvements in telecommunications obviated the need for local telegraph services. Although business telex services remained popular they too were overtaken in the early eighties by facsimile machines using telephone lines. Centralized service centers were subsequently established by the railways that could be reached by toll-free telephone lines and that was satisfactory for carload shippers, who consigned the bulk of the shipments placed with the railways. Mobile field representatives supplemented the role of the new centralized service centres.

By the time Canadian National began to consolidate its local agents into major centres, (Canadian Pacific had already done this by the seventies) the agent was almost an anachronism. Most of them had ceased to play a direct role in serving customers to any substantial degree and devoted most of their time to operational matters. Station agents had long issued train order authorities along "dark" lines, i.e., those that did not have electronic signals for communication between train dispatchers and the crews aboard the trains. Where such lines existed, the agent would place written train orders on a hoop that would be raised up to the cab of a passing train and from which the passing engineer would reach out and retrieve the orders. In this way, the flow of train traffic was controlled. By the early eighties, this method of train control was fast disappearing in favour of electronic and radiocommunication controls, although it still existed in some places[10]. The station agent had thus become redundant on the modern railway.

So too had the stations themselves, although in certain locations passenger train services continued, and platforms, or passenger shelters, were required for loading and the comfort of passengers. The main problem with the station buildings, however, was their potential heritage value. Usually, they were amongst the oldest buildings in a community and efforts were often made to preserve them. Although the Commission pronounced upon the fate of station buildings, it was without authority to order the railway companies to retain them for heritage reasons. Many historic railway structures were lost to their communities because they no longer possessed an operational purpose and their cost of acquisition and relocation could not be justified by the local government.

The CTC Western Division held a few hearings into major station agencies and station-building rationalizations in northern Manitoba and northern Alberta. There was local opposition to some of the rationalization proposals but nothing approaching the opposition that existed to branch-line abandonment. Local sentiments reflected the view of the railway as a public utility and were melodramatically expressed by the Cranberry Portage Chamber of Commerce which told the Commission (WDR1985-01, pg. 8):

> The agent is a person who understands the background and the individual needs of the local people. The agent is a member of the community, a guardian of the luggage and freight, an interpreter of the rules, a babysitter, a counselor, a tourist guide and a host in cold or wet weather. In effect, the agent is the human touch or quality of that cold machine called the CN.

---

10. I saw the old method used once while I was riding in the engine of a passenger train passing through 'dark' (i.e. non-signaled) territory in southern Alberta. An agent 'hooped up' the train orders to our engineer as we slowly passed the station platform.

However, the evidence almost always showed that the agent was redundant. Only once, at Lloydminster, did the evidence show that the Edmonton Service Centre was not providing a substitute service, and the agent was ordered to be maintained for a transitional period. Concerning passenger facilities, stations were ordered removed where suitable shelters could be put in place to meet the needs of the traveling public. The CTC Western Division was sympathetic to the loss of important heritage resources (a particular concern of Commissioner Wolfe, who had a long history in municipal government in Manitoba). However, there was simply no power under the *Railway Act* for the Commission to intervene and prevent the removal of a station building on heritage grounds. Later, specific legislation under the administration of the Department of the Environment was passed to deal with heritage stations and it provided at least a partial public-policy solution to the problem.

Another railway service that was once common but which quietly disappeared during the eighties was the transportation of cattle. When I first arrived in Saskatoon, it was still common to see cattle cars spotted on sidings at Intercontinental Packers on 11th Street, where there were holding pens and loading chutes. Within a few short years, however, all of the cattle traffic moved to motor transport, and the cattle cars and other infrastructure simply disappeared from the West.

CHAPTER 4.

BRANCH LINE EXPERIMENTS

In 1984 the Liberal government of John Turner was defeated in a general election but the coming into office of a Progressive Conservative administration under Brian Mulroney did not signal any alteration to the speed or orientation of change in the western grain transportation system. If anything, the national policy now advanced further toward an economically efficient Western transportation system. The CTC Western Division was asked by the new government to head up a formal inquiry into railway branch lines in Canada.

The *Inquiry Into Railway Branch Lines* was formally established by Order in Council P.C. 1984-4145 dated December 20, 1984, requiring the CTC Western Division to conduct an Inquiry focused on short-line railways, off-track elevators, and the Prairie Branch Line Rehabilitation Program. In addition to Commissioners McDonough and Wolfe, two Commissioners from the CTC's national headquarters, Commissioners Robert J. Orange, and David H. Chapman were added to the Inquiry.

A series of meetings with stakeholders was held throughout western Canada, although the commissioners decided against holding open public hearings. The Inquiry focused particularly on local modes of grain transportation that could be an alternative to traditional CN or CP branch line transportation systems. In its report, the inquiry did two things of importance. Firstly, it identified the lack of economic incentives for users of the transportation system as a barrier to change in Western transportation policy. Secondly, the inquiry provided a basis for promoting new transportation alternatives for the movement of grain in the West.

As a result, three alternative transportation experiments were devised to encourage new methods of grain handling and transportation. The first experiment consisted of an off-track elevator project in the Interlake region of Manitoba. The second project was a conventional short-line railway project in central Alberta and the last project was an unconventional short-line railway project using road/rail equipment in southern Saskatchewan.

The CTC Western Division worked closely with the Grain Transportation Agency (GTA), headquartered in Winnipeg on the Interlake off-track elevator project. The GTA was a short-lived regulatory agency primarily concerned with the movement of grain cars but was also responsible for promoting efficiencies in the grain handling and transportation system.

The CTC Western Division's experience with off-track elevators was derived from the consequences of an earlier abandonment order issued for the CP Melfort Subdivision in Saskatchewan. In that case, a bridge on the line had been rendered unusable and train operations were suspended long before the abandonment order became effective. To avoid hardship to local producers, the Commission authorized subsidy payments for both the grain hauls from the elevator located on the isolated segment of track to an elevator located on a neighboring branch line that had rail service, as well as the second elevation charges incurred at the second elevator until the date that the abandonment order became effective. That, in effect, was an off-track elevator scenario.

For the Interlake project, the abandonment of the CN Inwood Subdivision was deferred. Service to the Manitoba Pool elevators at Fisher Branch and Broad Valley by the CN were terminated, and arrangements were made to truck grain deliveries made at both Fisher Branch and Broad Valley to an elevator located on the neighboring CP Arborg Subdivision. The project was officially opened on September 12, 1986.

Off-track elevators incurred two costs that were not incurred by regular elevator operations along railway lines. Firstly, they incurred the trucking cost from the off-track elevator to the second elevator located on an adjacent rail line. Secondly, they incurred a second elevation charge at the elevator located on the serviced rail line. The cost savings from not operating the disused rail line was a net benefit arising from the project. However, it was necessary to balance those savings against the additional costs arising from trucking and elevation, and the subsequent movement of the grain out by rail from the second elevation point.

The Interlake off-track elevator project showed that cost savings could be obtained through this alternative but those savings would be offset by additional transfer costs. Although dramatic savings in costs could not be obtained, the off-track elevator concept was shown to have some use as an interim rationalization measure, particularly where the existing elevator facilities were in good shape and could last for quite several years with only running repairs. By the end of the eighties, as a result of this experiment, off-track elevators were operating on two other lines, the CN Acadia Valley Subdivision, and the CP Furness Subdivision, both in Alberta. Funding to support the off-track elevators was made available from the system improvement reserve fund under the *Western Grain Transportation Act*.

The second experiment involved the creation of a conventional short-line railway in central Alberta. A short-line railway consists of a private entity separate from a mainline railway that acquires a disused rail line and operates it as a local railway, usually without the mainline labour agreements that were commonly derived through collective bargaining between the mainline railway and its unions. It was a form of privatization and outsourcing of railway services. The business theory was that small, non-union firms could react more quickly and provide better local services correlated with the needs of local shippers than the large national railways. Thus, a short-line operation (it was hoped) could generate a profit where the mainline railways could not.

The CN Stettler Subdivision in Alberta was chosen for this experiment and it was an ideal line on which to attempt this concept. The Stettler Subdivision had been used by Via Rail's Rail Diesel Car (RDC) passenger train service[1] between Edmonton and Calgary before those passenger train services were discontinued and thus the trackage was in good physical condition, even though it was only 60 lb. rail. Secondly, there was a willing promoter of a short-line railway on this line waiting in the wings, Tom Payne, who had a dream to own a railway.

I first met Tom Payne in June 1984, when he came to see me at my office in Saskatoon to learn about the regulatory structure for railways in Canada. He was an engineer by training and had a great love of the railway industry. His passion to own and operate a railway impressed many public and private sector officials during the eighties.

Mr. Payne had selected the CN Stettler Subdivision as an ideal line on which to establish a short-line railway. Unfortunately, the CTC Western Division had previously held a public hearing about the Stettler Subdivision and had ordered CN to abandon the line. Conveniently, a one-year reprieve from the abandonment was granted by the CTC's Review Committee, as a result of a recent fire at an elevator located on the line. That reprieve allowed opponents of the abandonment led by the Red Deer

---

1. An RDC is a type of self-propelled railway carriage. They were manufactured by the Budd company in the United States.

Regional Planning Commission headed by Paul Meyette to launch a petition to the Governor General in Council to forestall the abandonment of the line.

At this time the short-lived administration of Prime Minister John Turner came to power and was casting about for new transportation policy initiatives. The government seized on the potential of using the Stettler Subdivision as a potential short-line experiment by taking the unusual step of granting the petition and issuing a formal reference under the *National Transportation Act* to the Commission requiring the CTC Western Division to hear and report back to the Governor General in Council on all issues relating to the abandonment of the Stettler Subdivision.

The reference hearing took place in the autumn of 1984 by which time the Turner Ministry had been replaced by a new government under Prime Minister Brian Mulroney. Tom Payne appeared as a witness to promote the option of a short-line railway on the Stettler line. Both CN and CP appeared skeptical of the concept, however, and the final report of the CTC Western Division only mentioned the short-line option in passing. However, the incoming Progressive Conservative government was interested in new approaches to the problems of the grain handling and transportation system, and that interest led to the subsequent *Inquiry Into Railway Branch Lines*. By the time the final report of that Inquiry was issued the short-line concept proposed for the Stettler Subdivision by Tom Payne had ripened.

The creation of what was subsequently named the Central Western Railway resulted from the involvement of several individuals and groups. Firstly, there was the Canadian National, which was the current owner of the line, and which remained skeptical of the potential for success of a short line option. The CN was cautious about the possibility of a sale of its line instead of its physical abandonment. Secondly, there was Tom Payne and his group in the Central Western Railway Corporation who were enthusiastic, though inexperienced, but who were expertly advised by a solid team of business lawyers from the Edmonton law firm of Milner Steer, headed by Rob Fulton and Tom Wakeling. Thirdly, there was the CTC Western Division, which was a neutral source of expertise, and Commissioner McDonough who had recently headed up the *Inquiry Into Railway Branch Lines*. In the background were policy officials in the Department of Transport in Ottawa, provincial officials in Edmonton, and trade union officials and their lawyers.

In establishing new short-line railways in Canada in the mid-eighties a promoter faced several legal questions. Firstly, there were transactional issues around how to create a short-line railway from a mainline railway. Secondly, within whose jurisdiction would a short-line railway fall – the federal government or a provincial government? And lastly, what would happen to the existing labour union contracts that had been entered into by the mainline railway? All three of these issues were interrelated and how one was resolved invariably affected the answer to one or both of the other questions. Amongst the practising Railway Bar in the West, these topics were of much interest and naturally resulted in differing views.

A lease of a branch line from a mainline railway would allow a short-line operator to operate a railway but there was a risk that the courts might conclude that a short-line railway company that leased its facilities from a mainline railway was more or less an agent for the main line railway company. As an agent of a federal work and undertaking a short-line railway company in that position would likely be found by the courts to be within federal jurisdiction. Since a short-line operator that leased its line would be unlikely to escape from federal jurisdiction there would be little economic incentive to promote the short-line railway option as either a reasonable business proposition or a potential solution to branch line abandonments.

Alternatively, perhaps by acquiring a branch line outright through a purchase and sale agreement a new short-line railway company could be severed from federal jurisdiction, and thus escape from the restrictive labour agreements under which the mainline carrier operated. Experience in the United States had shown that the key to having a successful short-line operation was operational flexibility and not necessarily lower wages. Moving short-line railway staff through different functional areas was essential. On any given day an employee on an American short-line could find himself or herself working in various capacities track-side, on a train, or perhaps even in the business office. Traditional railway labour agreements emphasized the specialization of labour, which made sense in a large industrial undertaking but that precluded labour flexibility as an aspect of mainline railway operations.

However, there was no clear jurisprudence to support the proposition that a purchase and sale of a branch line owned by a mainline railway would release that branch line from federal jurisdiction, and thus avoid the transference to a short-line railway of a mainline carrier's obligations to its labour unions. In the absence of any severance of federal jurisdiction, the *Canada Labour Code*[2] provided for the devolution of existing labour contracts where a business was sold as a going concern. That would certainly be the case if an operating branch line was sold to a short-line railway company that remained under federal jurisdiction.

A third impediment to establishing short-line railways on existing branch lines of a federally regulated railway company in the mid-eighties was that all of the physical works of the railway companies subject to federal jurisdiction had been declared by Parliament to be works for the general advantage of Canada under various legislation. The effect of such parliamentary dec-

---

2. *Canada Labour Code* RSC 1985, L-2

larations meant that for constitutional law purposes, all of the physical works and undertakings of the mainline carriers became subject to federal jurisdiction regardless of whether those physical works and undertakings crossed an interprovincial or international border (which was the ordinary method by which the federal government obtained its jurisdiction over a transportation company).

Declarations of general advantage to Canada had been made by Parliament in many railway statutes, including the *Railway Act* itself, during the great era of railway expansion in the late nineteenth and early twentieth centuries. Such declarations served to bring almost all railways in Canada under federal jurisdiction. The existence of a declaration covering a branch line of the CN or the CP meant that notwithstanding anything else a new short-line railway might remain within federal jurisdiction even if it was wholly contained within the boundaries of a single province, and otherwise constituted an independent enterprise.

Apart from these serious legal issues, a promoter of short-line options on the Canadian prairie in the mid-eighties had to be sensitive to the perspectives of the grain elevator companies, which were nervous about the prospect of trading known business partners (such as the mainline carriers, CN and CP) for unknown entities in the form of short-line railways. On grain-dependent branch lines, it was essential to retain the business confidence of the grain elevator companies to ensure the success of any short-line experiment. For example, in the case of the CN Stettler Subdivision, any suggestion that the CN might abandon the Stettler Subdivision and that rail service would be restored at some point in the future by a new operator unconnected to the CN might have prompted the elevator companies to surrender their elevator licenses and withdraw from the line. The timing of any transaction, the operational capacities of any new short-line railway, and the early commencement of operations by a new operator were all critical business considerations in establishing a new short-line railway on the prairie.

Ultimately, in the case of the CN Stettler Subdivision, the Central Western promoters elected to acquire the branch line from the CN by entering into a purchase and sale agreement in respect of the Stettler subdivision, taking over the railway branch line business as a going concern, and thereby accepting the jurisdictional risks. In the autumn of 1986, Central Western made a formal offer to CN to purchase the right of way and lands lying between mile 1.75 and mile 106.5 of the Stettler Subdivision. Canadian National accepted that offer and on November 20, 1986, the Governor General in Council approved the purchase and sale transaction under Section 23 of the *Canadian National Railways Act*[3]. The title of the line was transferred from Canadian National to Central Western on November 21, 1986. The first CWR train traversed the line on November 23, 1986.

---

3. *Canadian National Railways Act* RSC 1985, c. C-19

A souvenir ticket marking the commencement of the Central Western Railway

Central Western had previously acquired locomotives to move grain cars along the line and to spot them at the existing grain elevators. An interchange agreement with the CN was entered into under which empty grain cars were received by Central Western at Fellow Junction (located at the north end of the line) and returned loaded to that point. Canadian National was then responsible for taking the loaded cars to a destination seaport. In the meantime, another agreement was entered into by Central Western with the federal government under section 59 of the *Western Grain Transportation Act* and under that agreement, Central Western was able to obtain payment at the statutory rate basis for the movement of grain cars along the Central Western line. In addition to the grain business, the promoters also hoped to stimulate other business along the line including a steam tourist train operation. Regular operations by the new Central Western Railway began on December 2, 1986, when the first empty grain cars were spotted along the track for loading.

The creation of the Central Western Railway as an operational railway did not still the issue of which level of government would ultimately have legal jurisdiction over the line. With the jurisprudence not providing a clear answer the Commission took the view that earlier declarations by Parliament that the assets of Canadian National Railways were works for the general advantage of Canada could not be terminated by a sale of the line and thus the Central Western Railway would remain under federal jurisdiction. As that was contrary to the intentions of the promoters, they applied to the CTC Western Division in May 1987, requesting that the Commission invoke its rarely used power to state a case on a point of law to the Federal Court of Appeal. The CTC Western Division heard that application in an oral hearing in August 1987, (which proved to be its last public hearing). Tom Wakeling, counsel for Central Western, noted that there currently was a case concerning the constitutional jurisdiction over the Central Western before the Federal Court on appeal from the Canada Labour Relations Board (CLRB) involving CN's unions. Nevertheless, Wakeling argued that it would be appropriate for the CTC to state a case to the Federal Court.

Firstly, he argued that the CLRB case could become moot and the issue could thus remain an open one and, secondly, a stated case would provide an opportunity for the parties to supplement the existing record to assist the Court. Wakeling's arguments were countered by Douglas Wray, counsel for the railway unions, who argued that the CTC Western Division should not become involved in an existing proceeding before another federal tribunal. Ultimately, his arguments held the most appeal for the commissioners, who ruled that comity between federal boards and commissions required the CTC Western Division to refrain from exercising its power to state a case on a matter that was already proceeding before the Court from a decision of another federal tribunal.

Eventually, the Federal Court of Appeal heard the case on appeal from a decision of the Canada Labour Relations Board and decided that the Central Western Railway was indeed subject to the jurisdiction of Parliament. At least one of the judges who found in favour of federal jurisdiction decided the case in part based on the declarations of general advantage to Canada applicable to the CN's lines. An application was then subsequently brought by the Central Western Railway Corporation for leave to appeal to the Supreme Court of Canada and that application was granted.

In the meantime however, Parliament acted by amending the *Railway Act* to provide that a declaration that a particular work was a work of general advantage to Canada, or two or more provinces, would not continue to apply to any line of a railway that had been divested to a short-line railway. That legislation was made retroactive to include the acquisition of the CN Stettler Subdivision by the Central Western Railway. Thus, when the appeal came on for a hearing before the Supreme Court of Canada, the issue of a declaration was no longer present and the Court examined the constitutional question solely on the factual elements. In a landmark 1990 decision, the Supreme Court decided that the Central Western Railway was subject to the jurisdiction of the province rather than the federal government because the railway was located and operated solely within the confines of Alberta. The fact that the traffic carried by the Central Western Railway found its way into export commerce in no way affected the jurisdiction of the line. The provisions of the *Canada Labour Code* were not effective in devolving federal labour agreements onto a provincial short-line railway. Central Western Railway was thus free of both federal regulatory oversight and the restrictiveness of the federal labour agreements.

A committee was subsequently formed under the leadership of the Grain Transportation Agency, to examine whether the short-line railway concept made sense in the context of the western grain handling and transportation system. It would be fair to say that short-line railways in the highly regulated context of Canadian grain transportation did not provide significant overall cost savings, although there were some savings. Nevertheless, short lines did maintain service to communities that would have otherwise lost their rail service and they could provide a more efficient local service. Within a few years, other short lines would be created and would become a means of saving some lines (particularly those that could carry a reasonable amount of resource traffic). Short lines proved to be a sometimes viable alternative method to abandonment as a means of rationalizing the services provided by the mainline railways.

In 1990, an opportunity arose for the CTC's successor, the National Transportation Agency to review the progress of the Central Western Railway. Canadian Pacific proposed to transfer its Coronation and Lacombe Subdivisions, traversing central Alberta in an east and west direction, to the new Central Western Railway. The transfer drew together themes of rationalization without abandonment, lower cost alternatives to abandonment, short lines, and service levels[4].

Public interest issues played the largest role in the hearing. The Agency found that it had to:

> ... weigh the impact of the proposed sale to CWR on such matters as: the impact of the operations of CWR on individuals, businesses, labour, and the economic development of the Coronation/Lacombe region; the financial and economic prospects of the CWR railway operation; and the ability of CWR to operate as part of an economic, efficient and adequate transportation network.[5]

---

4. I did not personally participate in this proceeding but two of our NTA Western Region economists, Roy Proctor and Brian Gill, attended the hearing and advised the Agency members on the economic issues.
5. NTA Decision *Re Transfer of the Coronation and Lacombe Subdivisions.*

In this hearing, major public interest issues raised within these broad considerations included: common carrier obligations, prohibition order survival, rail service, incentive rates, the impact of a transfer on system costs and rates, the financial strength of CWR, labour, and any other issue affecting the grain transportation system, including trucking considerations, and the method of payment of a transport subsidy.

Some of the public interest interveners who appeared at this hearing were worried that a transfer of lines to the CWR would place many Alberta producers in a riskier position concerning service than they would be in if the line remained with the CP. Between the time the hearing was held and the issuance of the Agency's decision however, the Supreme Court of Canada handed down its landmark judgement in *United Transportation Union v Central Western Railway Corp*[6], which decided that the CWR was subject to provincial jurisdiction. As such, the federal common carrier obligations given statutory force by the *National Transportation Act 1987* were held to be no longer applicable. Nevertheless, the Agency was able to find that analogous provisions of the *Railway Act* of Alberta offered shippers comparable protection. Although the Coronation and Lacombe Subdivisions had been subject to Prohibition Orders, it was clear that with the sundering of federal jurisdiction, those orders would lapse. Nevertheless, some analogous protection was offered by the transfer agreement itself, which stipulated that CP could reacquire the line under certain conditions, or if the CWR became financially insolvent.

The evidence presented at the hearing respecting the level of service available to producers located within the economic catchment area of the Coronation and Lacombe subdivisions was very much in CWR's favour. Evidence concerning CWR's operations on the former Stettler Subdivision of Canadian National showed

---

6. *United Transportation Union v Central Western Railway Corp.*, [1990] 3 SCR 1112.

that the short-line had increased service levels far above those of the former mainline railway. Faster service drew more grain deliveries to the elevators located on the CWR and boosted the overall tonnage handled by the line. By every measure relating to service, the CWR was a success.

The most interesting part of the case revolved around the impact of the transfer on the costs of the entire grain handling and transportation system. This was a complex issue, as the Western grain subsidy program was extremely intricate. Alberta Wheat Pool, represented once again by its veteran counsel, Marshall Rothstein QC, was opposed to a transfer that resulted in higher short-line costs than the cost reduction to the system that would be obtained by the transfer. The Pool was also vexed by the fact that CWR carried higher risks than the CP and that uncertainty existed concerning the cost scenario for the transferred lines after the next quadrennial costing review under the *Western Grain Transportation Act.*

Some participants argued for a policy approach that had first been given prominence in the *Inquiry Into Railway Branch Lines Report,* namely, that a comparative approach should be employed and the lowest cost alternative chosen. Where a short-line was clearly the lowest cost option then it would be selected. However, where a trucking option, perhaps utilizing off-track elevators, would provide a lower-cost alternative then that was the option that should be selected.

While the new *National Transportation Act 1987* did pick up on that theme and provided a legislative mechanism for funding lower-cost rationalization alternatives, there was no legislated integration of that mechanism into the provision of the public subsidies available under another statute. Thus, any funds for a lower-cost alternative would have to be obtained from outside the existing financial framework. As the overall budgetary situation facing the federal government in the late eighties was alarming, this was simply not an option that the government could contemplate.

In any event, the short-line alternative to rationalization had proved its worth, at least in the context of the Central Western Railway. The inhabitants of the region affected by the transfer to a short-line enjoyed increased service levels, and the mainline railways were able to escape local situations that were not economic for them. Further, a transfer of the lines meant that the provincial governments need not be concerned about increased road cost burdens and the federal government could take comfort from the fact that all of the other interests were satisfied. In early January 1991, the Agency approved the transfer of the Coronation and Lacombe subdivisions, thus confirming the success of the rail rationalization alternative strategies which had taken shape in the mid-eighties[7].

At the end of the century, Central Western Railway had expanded and had then become part of a major short-line operator originally from the United States, known as Rail America. Changes to federal subsidies for grain transportation eventually led to further consolidations and further rail rationalization, even with respect to short-line railways. Much of the original Stettler branch line was abandoned by the CWR on July 31, 1997. However, the CWR experiment proved that short-line railways were a viable option in Canada and that they could be alternatives to branch-line abandonments.

The third experimental project resulting from the work of the *Inquiry Into Railway Branch Lines* involved the use of road-railer equipment on disused branch lines. The federal government provided funding for this experiment under the WGTA's system improvement reserve fund but it was sponsored largely by the Government of Saskatchewan. The road-rail equipment consisted of a specially designed vehicle that was capable of move-

---

7. The transaction was not finalized until 1992.

ment over roads under its own power but could also travel on railway lines because it had special rail wheels. The experiment was operated on the CP Colony subdivision and the CN Avonlea Subdivision in southern Saskatchewan. The road-railer moved from line to line by highway and then traversed the rail lines from a junction point picking up empty grain cars for spotting at the elevators located along the line. In true Saskatchewan fashion, a cooperative association, the Southern Rails Co-op, was established amongst producers along the Colony and Avonlea branch lines as the legal vehicle for the provision of this service. Service commenced in June 1990.

As the experiments which grew out of the *Inquiry Into Railway Branch Lines* began to be planned the CTC Western Division completed its last branch line abandonment hearings. In the case of both the CN Porter Subdivision in central Saskatchewan and the CN Corning Subdivision in southern Saskatchewan the CTC Western Division reconsidered the status of two lines that it had earlier ordered the CN to continue to operate. Although both lines were in poor condition and did not warrant further retention the efforts being made to create viable alternatives to branch line abandonment through various experiments persuaded the Commission to order both lines retained. The Commission also directed that local committees should be established to look into the creation of alternatives to rationalization at the delivery points on both of those lines.

The hearing into the abandonment of the Corning Subdivision, heard at Peebles, Saskatchewan on August 21, 1986, proved to be the last public hearing into the abandonment of a prairie grain dependent branch line, ending a decades-old process. Within a brief time during the eighties the processes of branch line rationalization had been successfully integrated into the evolution of the grain handling and transportation system.

CHAPTER 5.

URBAN RELOCATIONS

One area of railway rationalization that did meet with general approval in the West during this era concerned urban rail rationalization. Though railways were once essential to the life of every Western community, they were of less economic importance by the eighties. Nevertheless, many Western cities found the railways occupying prime land in downtown cores. Urban renewal warranted many cities trying to remove the railway yards that interfered with modern urban pursuits. Hence the interest in railway diversion and relocation projects.

In a few cases, the railways found it economically advantageous to voluntarily relocate their rail yard facilities. Saskatoon was the prime example of the beneficial effects of rail line relocation. The removal of the central yard of Canadian National allowed the construction of the Mid-Town Mall, which contributed to the overall improvement of the downtown core of the city. The City of Lethbridge in Alberta had also been successful in negotiating a railway relocation project for that community. Several consensual orders were issued by the CTC Western Division to facilitate that project and our engineers monitored the progress of the Lethbridge relocation, which was generally considered to be a success.

Difficulties emerged when the railway and the community could not come to terms concerning relocation or diversion projects. The railways naturally sought financial incentives to relocate their facilities but some communities could not, or would not, devise a financial package that was attractive to the railways. In other cases, some communities complained that they could not come to terms with a railway and were left with no recourse because railways were under federal jurisdiction and their lands could not be expropriated. As a result of those complaints, a statute known as the *Railway Relocation and Crossing Act* (RRCA)[1] was enacted by Parliament.

The RRCA provided a complex method of arranging for the removal of railway facilities from urban communities. The RRCA provided a compulsory mechanism to remove rail lines without creating economic incentives for the railways to do so voluntarily. Thus, under the RRCA, a railway company was to be placed in a no better or no worse position than it previously occupied. In practice, it proved almost impossible to conclusively establish whether the railways were in a no-better or no-worse position following a relocation project.

The testing ground for the RRCA was the City of Regina, Saskatchewan. The Queen City, as it was called, had long desired to remove the Canadian National yards from the center of the City together with parts of the CN Craik Subdivision and the CN Central Butte Subdivision. The Canadian Pacific Lanigan Subdivision was also proposed for relocation.

The railways objected to the proposed relocation and raised every obstacle to prevent it. Ultimately, the railways were unsuccessful in their attempts to stop the proceedings and were compelled to join issue with the city on the main application. But not before they twice took the CTC Western Division to the Federal Court Trial Division seeking prerogative relief to stop the hearing process. And twice they took the CTC Western Division to the Federal Court of Appeal, once on an appeal from the Trial Division, and once seeking leave to appeal the CTC Western Division's ultimate decision in the matter, as well as making one application to the Supreme Court of Canada. Veteran advo-

---

1. *Railway Relocation and Crossing Act* R.S.C. 1970, c. R-4.

cate Marshall Rothstein QC argued the case for the City while CN and CP used their Winnipeg-based lawyers Grant Nerbas and Winston Smith. I participated in all of the superior court litigation and in the regulatory hearings in my usual capacity.

A fifty-three-day public hearing in Regina resulted in the approval of the rail relocation project but the delays, as well as the outcome of some of the specific economic regulatory judgements made by the CTC Western Division ultimately increased the costs of the project beyond 100 million dollars, and that proved in the end to be too costly for the City to undertake, even with a federal grant in excess of twenty million dollars.

The Regina experience may have discouraged other municipalities from following the same path instead of opting for a negotiated agreement with the railway companies. With negotiations, a municipality could incorporate financial incentives that could encourage the railways to cooperate in the relocation of their yards and other facilities.

Following the release of the Regina Rail Relocation decision the City of Saskatoon began to examine the rail lines that continued to dissect that city. The new focusing Saskatoon was the CP yard located on the outskirts of the downtown core, as well as CP and CN lines in the east and west halves of the City. Saskatoon lobbied the Minister of Transport for assistance and the Minister instructed the new National Transportation Agency to conduct an inquiry under the *National Transportation Act 1987.* That became a joint project of Agency headquarters in Hull, Quebec, and the NTA Western Region in Saskatoon. The NTA Western Region supplied the technical team for the project including the railway engineering, operating, and dispute resolution expertise, while our headquarters provided its expertise in economics.

However, neither railway was interested in moving any of their remaining facilities out of their existing locations in Saskatoon.

Thus the final Inquiry Report merely discussed the technical layout of the railway lines in Saskatoon and the economics of relocation. Since there was no federal money for rail line relocation in Saskatoon the City itself could not afford the cost. However, the City did change its zoning bylaws as a result of the Inquiry to protect the existing rail line corridors from development in the future if the railways voluntarily vacated their rail corridor lands in Saskatoon.

In 1986, I served as counsel to the Commission at a hearing held in Vancouver to implement the preferred method of diverting dangerous commodities traffic from the CP Coal Harbour Yard on the Vancouver waterfront. The hearing was a continuation of a series of proceedings that examined the movement of dangerous commodities traffic through Vancouver. The matter became urgent as a result of the planned holding of Expo 86 along the Vancouver waterfront. The former Pier B-C was taken over to form the base of the new Canada Pavilion which ultimately would become the Vancouver cruise ship terminal. At the time Coal Harbour was the site of a significant CP yard and the mainland departure and return point for Vancouver Island-bound dangerous commodities rail traffic. There was a real urgency to move the outbound dangerous commodities traffic out of the Coal Harbour area in preparation for Expo 86, which was intended to be a regional and national showcase. The presence of dangerous commodities traffic raised significant issues of public safety and security for the promoters of the world exposition and the federal and provincial governments. The Commission heard evidence on three alternatives, the use of the Burlington Northern Railroad (BN) ferry slip in east Vancouver, the Seaspan ferry slip located on the British Columbia Railway in North Vancouver, and the ferry slips located at Squamish on the British Columbia Railway.

None of the alternatives was ideal but the use of Burlington Northern's facilities continued to make the most sense from a practical perspective given the exigencies of time and the fact that the Commission could exercise jurisdiction over the BN facilities (the British Columbia Railway was subject to provincial jurisdiction). The Commission reaffirmed the BN ferry slip as its preferred choice for the outbound movement of dangerous commodities traffic from Vancouver and confirmed that outbound traffic must be re-routed over the BN facilities before the commencement of Expo 86. The Commission also called for regional planning to be undertaken by the province, municipalities, and the railways to effect a long-term solution to the problem of movements of dangerous commodities through Vancouver. Ultimately, after the successful Expo 86[2], the entire Coal Harbour area was redeveloped for urban uses and it became a coveted address, with many high-priced condominiums lining the Vancouver waterfront area.

Another significant urban rationalization project occurred in Edmonton, Alberta in 1989. Canadian National applied for permission to relocate its Edmonton City Yard and a portion of the Edson Subdivision to release lands for redevelopment. The prime subject of the redevelopment was to be a new downtown campus for Grant McEwan College. Since I had gained expertise in railway relocations and diversions the new National Transportation Agency appointed me as an Inquiry Officer under section 32 of the *National Transportation Act 1987*, and I proceeded to hold a public inquiry into the proposed relocation.

In Edmonton, the CN proposed to remove two main tracks from its main station to a point west of 116th Street and to remove its City Yard trackage. The CN/CP interchange would be relocated from the City Yard to a point outside the City at the Clover Bar interchange. In addition to the making of track changes to accommodate passenger train operations by Via Rail, CN also proposed to construct 3.3 miles of new mainline track from Bev-

---

2. Including a very successful Steam Expo which brought several surviving working steam locomotives to Vancouver in conjunction with Expo 86.

erly Bridge to the Calder Yard Entry/Exit line and within Calder Yard to construct a new yard office building, new wrap-around tracks, and an extension of the 97th Avenue subway. Finally, CN proposed the construction of industrial support yard trackage within its Bissell yard and the re-designation of its main line trackage as an industrial spur near the West Junction of the Edson Subdivision.

Canadian National gave notice to all of its shippers within a thirty-kilometre radius of the City Yard interchange. On May 31, 1989, I convened a public inquiry in a hotel in downtown Edmonton. Lawyers representing CN, CP, and Via were present, along with representatives of the Province of Alberta, the cities of Edmonton and Spruce Grove, economic and tourism development authorities, and various shippers. Both CN and Via dispatched Vice-Presidents to attend the Inquiry. Ms. Wendy Tadros of the NTA headquarters legal office agreed to act as counsel to the Inquiry. In addition, several other officers from the NTA Western Division and the NTA headquarters office provided support.

I opted for a less formal approach in the conduct of this public inquiry proceeding. To promote openness I dispensed with sworn evidence and transcripts, although I made my notes of what the various parties said. There were four main issues to be addressed. Firstly, there was the issue of the redevelopment of the railway lands in the public interest. There was evidence to show that the removal of the City Yard and associated tracks would promote the public interest, particularly with the construction of the new college.

Secondly, concern was expressed by shippers that the relocation of the CN/CP interchange would put them outside of the thirty-kilometre interswitching limits, or at least put them into a higher rate zone, thus increasing their costs. Under the interswitching rules traffic in areas surrounding a junction between two railways can be transferred from one railway to the other at the order of the shipper for a flat fee. Interswitching promoted the efficient collection, movement, and delivery of traffic. Interswitching was divided into four zones within a thirty-mile radius of the junction, with higher payments required as the zones increased outwards from the physical connection point.

However, this issue was resolved when CN and CP agreed that they would absorb the incremental interswitching charges at Edmonton which resulted from the relocation, even though they were not obliged to do so by the strict letter of the law. Canadian National stated that it regarded its commitment to be in the nature of a public undertaking to the Inquiry. Given a public promise by the Applicant and the agreement between the two railways, it was clear that the interests of the shippers would be protected by this relocation.

Another concern over interswitching was the position of the neighbouring City of Spruce Grove. It was the desire of that municipality to develop its industrial park and Spruce Grove felt that it would be impeded in that desire since the relocation of the CN/CP interchange to Clover Bar would remove Spruce Grove from the prescribed interswitching limits. However, Canadian National indicated that it would consent to an order of the Agency to extend interswitching limits to include the Spruce Grove industrial park, which resolved that issue.

Another significant issue concerned the impact of the relocation on Via Rail's passenger train operations and tourism in Edmonton. The changes CN wanted to make would require Via passenger trains to make reverse movements into the station and that would add thirteen minutes to the existing passenger-train schedules. Although Via Rail initially expressed reservations about the Edmonton relocation project by the time the public inquiry was held Via stated that it no longer had any concerns.

Via's Vice President indicated that Via would accept the thirteen-minute incremental increase in its passenger train schedule.

Several public interest groups or institutions also appeared and provided evidence on public interest issues, including Transport 2000, the City of Edmonton, and Tourism Edmonton After assessing this evidence, I concluded that, on balance, the impacts on both passenger-train operations and on tourism in Edmonton were acceptable in consideration of the overall public benefits of the project.

Another issue concerned the re-designation of part of the existing mainline track to industrial spur status. The effect of this re-designation would be to remove the statutory protection that was afforded by the *National Transportation Act 1987* in respect of any future rationalization of the line. A number of the shippers located on this portion of the trackage were upset at the potential loss of their regulatory shield and CN attempted to meet their concerns by promising to notify them if and when the railway planned to rationalize this trackage. However, that would not necessarily provide the shippers with an effective recourse and would not protect any shippers who were located along that trackage in the future. I determined that all current and potential shippers should be placed on the same footing as existed at the time of the Inquiry with respect to the protections offered to them in connection with future rail rationalization. My report to the Agency ultimately suggested that the trackage in question be designated as auxiliary trackage to the Edson Subdivision, which would afford it statutory protection, and would avoid any potential discrimination in the provision of notices between current and future shippers.

The last issue that I had to deal with was the overall rail infrastructure and operating impacts. Here the evidence was very much in favour of the relocation. The new design diverted the main line around the Calder Yard rather than running through the center of the City Yard. Further, the construction of a wrap-around track would enhance operational flexibility in respect of yard operations, or yard bypass operations. Finally, new marshalling industrial trackage would be constructed in Bissell Yard and would provide additional yard operational capacity and flexibility. Based on the evidence, I found that the relocation would result in a good overall technical design.

My Inquiry Report was finalized on June 20, 1989, and I recommended that the Edmonton relocation project be approved by an Order of the Agency without any further formal hearings of the Agency. I also recommended that the Agency provide by order that the City of Spruce Grove Industrial Park be included within interswitching limits and that a small portion of the Edson Subdivision between the west limit of Calder Yard and 116th Street be designated as auxiliary trackage subject to rationalization control.

The Agency Board subsequently concurred with the conclusions of my report and approved the CN application except that they preferred to separate out the issue of the re-designation of Edson Subdivision trackage as auxiliary trackage and hold a subsequent proceeding to finalize that issue.[3]

No appeals were taken from this proceeding and the relocation order took effect. The lands freed by the reolocation were made available for the new college and it provided Edmonton with a significant public benefit.

---

3. *Re Application by the Canadian National Railway Company for Amendments to Plans, Profiles, and Books of Reference to facilitate trackage changes at Edomonton, Alberta,* (1989) N.T.A.R. 431 (NTA Decision and Inquiry Report)

PART III.

THE END OF THE CROWSNEST PASS FREIGHT RATE

CHAPTER 6.

SHADOWS OF THE PAST

In January 1982 the attention of the CTC Western Division was focused on the historic *Crowsnest Pass Act*[1] rate, or Crow Rate as it was colloquially known. First established in 1897 the Crow Rate represented a reduction of three cents per hundredweight on grain and flour shipped on the Canadian Pacific Railway from points in western Canada to the Lakehead (Port Arthur and Fort William, Ontario – now Thunder Bay, Ontario). The rates on certain manufactured items inbound to western Canadian destinations, which were required by settlers, were also reduced. In return, Canadian Pacific received a subsidy amounting to $3,400,000.00 for the construction of a railway line from Lethbridge, in what was then the Northwest Territories (and is now Alberta) to Nelson, in British Columbia.

The effect of the Crow Rate was to embed in a statute of Parliament an agreed-upon reduction in rates for movements of western grain out of western Canada, and a reduction in rates for movements into western Canada of goods for settlement without restriction in time. The effect was to spur the settlement of the West and to give confidence to the farming community that a major cost of doing business – the cost of rail transportation – would remain predictable.

In 1902, the Crow Rate actually fell below the maximum permitted under the agreement when a further agreement was entered into by the government of Manitoba with the Canadian Pacific

1. *Crowsnest Pass Act* 60-61 Vic. c. 5

Railway. There the matter rested until late in World War I when the financial strains on the Canadian railways (by then including, the Grand Trunk Pacific and the Canadian Northern Railway) proved to be too great for them to bear, and the Cabinet authorized an exemption from the Crow Rate under wartime emergency legislation. That exemption continued into the immediate postwar period which also saw major confrontations in Parliament and before the Board of Railway Commissioners between those advocating the need of western farmers for the restoration of the Crow Rate, and advocates of the need for the railways to achieve revenue adequacy. This was the conflict in perspectives that would animate the public debate between the railways and the grain producers through to the end of the twentieth century.

Ultimately, the Crow Rate was not only restored on outbound grain but it was also extended to cover the lines of the Canadian Pacific Railway constructed in the period after 1897, as well as all of the western lines of the Canadian National Railways (the Crown-owned successor to the Grand Trunk Pacific and the Canadian Northern Railway). The Crow Rate was also extended to include movements from western origins westward to Vancouver and Prince Rupert in recognition of the competition from the Panama Canal which had been constructed after the creation of the original Crow Rate. The position was summarized by the Board of Railway Commissioners in its judgement in the case of *Province of British Columbia* v *Canadian Freight Association* (1926), 30 C.R.C. 393 where it said:

> Though the Board has repeatedly held that rates to be just and reasonable, must be just and reasonable to the railways no less than to others concerned, Parliament has now decreed that irrespective, almost, of the cost of transportation [. . .] this national asset [grain and flour] must find its way to market, so far as railway carriage is concerned, at a rate substantially lower than other commodities bear. The enormous national

value of the grain production of Canada justifies such procedure.

There the matter rested through ensuing decades. By 1980 the Crow rate had become a sacred cow in western Canadian politics. The political fear of tampering with the Crow Rate can be seen during the debate on the enactment of the *National Transportation Act* in 1967 in which the then Minister of Transport, Jack Pickersgill, said:

> There is no intention whatever, indeed it is forbidden in this bill, to review the Crowsnest rates. They are frozen as hard as any legislation could possibly freeze them, for all time to come. We have even improved the situation by freezing them specifically for [the port of] Churchill[2].

Economic changes since 1897 however, had placed the railway companies and the government in a difficult position. Competition from highway transport had skimmed off the high-value commodities from the railways leaving the branch line network in the prairies largely devoted to the hauling of grain. However, as the grain rates were set by statute at the 1897 Crow Rate level there was no economic relationship between the costs of operation and the revenue derived from grain operations. Nor did the railway companies have any other realistic means of increasing their revenues from grain and thus they incurred substantial and unsupportable losses.

After 1967, the federal government established a subsidy program under the *Railway Act* to compensate the railways for the losses they incurred in the operation of uneconomic branch lines but the railways maintained that this program did not cover all of their economic losses and, in any event, it merely shifted the burden from railway shippers to the general population. Thus, pressure began to mount for changes to the Crow Rate.

2. *Debates of the House of Commons*, 1st Session, 27th Parliament, p. 11916

Early in 1982, the federal government made its opening gambit in the reform of the Crow Rate. Minister of Transport Jean-Luc Pepin announced that a University of Manitoba economist, Dr. Clay Gilson, would be given a mandate to review the Crow Rate. Predictably, an uproar resulted throughout western Canada. In January 1982 it was announced that Minister Pepin would come to Saskatoon and that he would speak outside the city, in the town of Delisle, Saskatchewan, at a meeting organized by the local Chamber of Commerce. I was asked to observe the meeting.

The meeting took place in the local arena in Delisle, Saskatchewan, with the Minister standing out on the carpet-covered ice and surrounded by several hundred grain producers filling the stands. Bravely, the Minister explained the case for change, the particular issues that Dr. Gilson and his team would explore, and the government's commitment to continue to pay total subsidies of $800 million, the largest subsidy in the federal budget. Specifically, Dr. Gilson would be asked to examine the proper level of compensation to the railways, whether payments should be made to the railways or grain producers, whether performance guarantees should be extracted from the railways, as well as the sensitive issue of variable freight rates.

Throughout the meeting, the Minister was treated to a denunciation of the government's policy intentions. For myself, it was an impressionable introduction to the issue of the Crow Rate and the resistance of the western grain-growing community to contemplate any changes to it. Nevertheless, I thought that there may have been an underlying current of resignation in the crowd, despite the denunciations. When Minister Pepin described how the current system was reducing the cost of transportation borne by western grain producers to the point where they would only bear 7% of the total costs by the mid-nineties, a noticeable segment of the crowd did not join in the general commotion and jeering that followed.

Later, back in Saskatoon, the Minister was swarmed by farmers as he attempted to cross the street outside the Bessborough Hotel in yet another foray into this contentious issue. In his game attempt to persuade the western grain farmers of the need for change, one could only admire the Minister's pluck.

Around this time opponents of change in Saskatoon painted a large crow on a white board which they paraded around town in the back of a truck as a beacon for a local petition drive against any change to the Crow Rate. For a while, the "cardboard crow" was a familiar sight around the city.

The Crow Rate also became important to me in a more specific context at this time. I now proceeded to act as counsel on what would prove to be the last major rate case involving the Crow Rate. The case of *Prairie Malt (Canada) Limited* v *Canadian National Railways* was an appeal by a barley malting firm in Biggar, Saskatchewan, which was engaged in the export of barley malt through West Coast ports. Prairie Malt had benefitted from a tariff issued by the Canadian National Railway Company which provided for the movement of barley malt from Biggar, Saskatchewan, to Pacific tidewater under the Crow Rate but the CN had tacked onto the Crow Rate an arbitrary rate for movements by ocean carriers via rail or highway transport to Seattle for the physical loading of the grain aboard a vessel.

This special arbitrary rate[3] allowed Prairie Malt to utilize ocean shipping firms doing business out of Vancouver even though their ships did not actually call at that port. This flexibility in access to shipping gave Prairie Malt the ability to sell abroad into new markets in the Far East and the Caribbean Sea. However, Canadian National had second thoughts about the precedent it had created by allowing the use of the Crow Rate for movements by rail that ultimately ended up being loaded onto

---

3. The expression "arbitrary rate" is a term of art and does not imply anything about the characteristics of the rate or the intentions of the railway company.

ships in Seattle, Washington, rather than in one of our own ports, and so the railway progressively increased the arbitrary charge from 20 cents per hundredweight to 61 cents per hundredweight in order to discourage the movements. When discouragement proved fruitless, the railway attempted to terminate the arbitrary outright (and thus with it the ability of Prairie Malt to access ocean lines calling at Seattle).

For me, the Prairie Malt case meant an immersion into the history of the Crow Rate and various legal proceedings and orders of the Board of Railway Commissioners that had been issued in the twenties during the last period of grain rate turmoil. In this case, the quorum of the CTC Western Division consisted of Commissioner McDonough and two commissioners from our eastern headquarters, Commissioner J.A.D. Magee, Chairman of the Commission's Railway Transport Committee, and Commissioner J.F. Walter, a future Chairman of the Railway Transport Committee. Since we lacked a suitable hearing room at the CTC Western Division office, the old Council Chamber of the City of Saskatoon Municipal Building was pressed into service.

Prairie Malt's appeal was handled by Marshall Rothstein QC and was supported by the Province of Saskatchewan, which retained a prominent Ottawa counsel, Francois Lemieux, for the case. The railways were represented by their in-house legal staff, Winnipeg-based Paul Antymniuk for Canadian National, and Marc Shannon for Canadian Pacific Limited.

The hearing was unusual in that it was cast as a determination of a preliminary point of law to ascertain whether the device of an arbitrary rate added onto the Crow Rate was legal. The railways argued that it was not legal because the traffic was not export grain since the movement of the grain did not terminate in Vancouver, as was required by the Crow Rate.

However, the CTC Western Division determined as a matter

of fact that all of the movements did terminated for rail transportation purposes in Vancouver. The CTC Western Division relied on one of its previous judgements (cited by Rothstein) in which the Commission had entreated the railways to treat all traffic that was identified as export traffic as export traffic, and not to attempt to create some kind of domestic-export hybrid in respect of the application of the Crow Rate.

Marshall Rothstein had argued that barley malt was a grain product and that the Canadian National Railway Company had taken financial assistance for the movement of grain in the form of subsidies for grain car purchases and the rehabilitation of railway box cars. Having taken the Queen's coin, the railway company was precluded by a special provision of the *Railway Act* from increasing the rates on westbound movements of grain products such as barley malt beyond the rate which was in force on December 31, 1966. However, the CTC Western Division demurred from that argument since it seemed to be a backdoor approach to the imposition of a statutory freight rate.

Rather, it was another argument of Messrs. Lemieux and Rothstein that the commissioners favoured. Lemieux and Rothstein argued that the movement fell within the parameters of *General Order 448* of the Board of Railway Commissioners, which had reapplied the Crow Rate in the 1920s, following the dislocations of the First World War, and which had subsequently been confirmed as the cornerstone of Crow Rate regime by another provision of the *Railway Act*.

This argument formed the main battlefield for counsel and the Commission had to wade through much law concerning whether barley malt was a grain, or a grain product, whether the words contained in the preamble to a legal document could affect the meaning to be attributed to the enacting clauses, and whether the plain and literal rule of statutory interpretation, or the golden rule of interpretation, should be applied to the interpretation of both the statute and the tariff.

The Commission eventually found in favour of Prairie Malt and in the salient portion of its decision stated:

> In this case, barley malt is railed to Vancouver where it is containerized and the containers are then transferred to the ocean carrier. The ocean carrier issues its ocean bill of lading showing the foreign destination of the containers. However, for reasons of commerce, the ocean carrier then makes arrangements for the transportation of the containers to Seattle where they are loaded aboard the ships for transportation abroad, instead of shifting the vessels into Vancouver to embark the containers. The fact that the ocean carrier finds it more convenient to rail or truck the containers to Seattle and embark them aboard its ships there does not alter the fact that this is grain moving to Vancouver for export. In our opinion, the requisites of [the *Railway Act* and General Order 448 of the Board of Railway Commissioners] are met by the applicant when it ships its barley malt to Vancouver by rail and turns the barley malt over to the ocean carrier for export abroad from Vancouver.[4].

The WGTA abolished the Crow Rate but it did not abolish the concept of a statutory rate for the carriage of grain. The new modernized statutory rate was, however, radically different from the Crow Rate in several particulars. The new statutory rate

---

4. CTC Western Division Decision: *In Re Prairie Malt*, 1982/footnote]
Thus, the last of many battles fought between grain shippers and the railways over the application of the Crow Rate ended in a victory for the shippers. Nevertheless, it was a short-lived victory for shippers for by this time the Gilson Task Force had released its report concerning the proposed replacement of the Crow Rate. The government moved quickly to abolish the Crow Rate based on Dr. Gilson's recommendations and replaced it with a considerably reformed statutory grain freight rate structure under the new *Western Grain Transportation Act* (WGTA)[5] *Western Grain Transportation Act* S.C. 1983-84, c. 13

5.

structure provided for a flexible rate structure and grain producers would have to pay more of the total cost of transportation, although the bulk of the cost would continue to be the responsibility of the federal treasury. The new rate structure would also allow for variable rates, an innovation bitterly contested by those who feared that it would expedite the abandonment of rural branch lines and thereby contribute to the loss of the grain-based rural society on the Prairie.

The government did not meet its timetable for the enactment of the *Western Grain Transportation Act* due to filibustering in Parliament by the opposition Progressive Conservatives and New Democrats. The delay in the passage of the legislation until late 1983 caused a significant legal problem in that the new Act called for the filing of new statutory rate tariffs to be filed no later than November 1, 1983. That date proved impossible to meet since the statute was not enacted until November 29, 1983. Opponents of the new legislation applied to the Commission's Railway Transport Committee, and subsequently to the Commission's Review Committee in Hull, Quebec, for an order setting aside the new statutory rate tariff filing. Both requests were denied on narrow legal grounds of interpretation. If they had been granted chaos would have resulted since the implementation of the new rate structure would have been delayed until August of 1984 but in the interim without the former Crow Rates which had been abolished only railway class rates, a type of backstop rate, could have applied. These backstop rates were higher than both the old Crow Rate and the new statutory rate and would likely have caused a firestorm of protest across the Prairie.

Not content with the rulings of the Commission, the National Farmers Union, a farm organization based in Saskatoon, took the issue to the Federal Court of Appeal. As the issue involved the interpretation of an Act of Parliament, the Commission asked the Department of Justice to assume responsibility for the case, which it did. When the appeal came on for hearing in Regina,

I was given the task of assisting the Justice Department's Chief General Counsel, Eric Bowie QC, in conducting the government's case. The Court dealt with the issue in short order, finding that the issue was a question of parliamentary intent and that the transitional provisions of the legislation allowed the Commission to accept tariff filings at a date later than the Act prescribed. Accordingly, the appeal was dismissed and the new Act was confirmed as fully operational. With this rocky start, the era of the *Crowsnest Pass Act* swept into history, and the grain handling and transportation system moved into the era of the *Western Grain Transportation Act* and its reformed rate structure.

The new grain rate structure was embedded in an extremely complex piece of financial legislation. Under it, the government and grain producers paid the railways for the cost of moving grain from points along main and branch lines in western Canada to ports at the Lakehead, Pacific tidewater, or Hudson Bay. While the government still paid the lion's share of the cost of transportation producers paid more than they would have under the *Crowsnest Pass Act* rates as adopted by the Board of Railway Commissioners in *General Order 448*. For the railways, the new rate system was a boon to their revenues. Now they could count on a statutory rate that actually compensated them for the operational costs of moving grain as well as guaranteeing them an approximately 20% return on the capital they invested in the movement of grain.

As always whenever new programs as complex as this one are implemented, there are many transitional problems and so the early part of 1984 saw the CTC Western Division engaged in adjudicating complaints concerning the application of the new tariff structure. In fact, the hearing of tariff complaints under the *Western Grain Transportation Act* became a frequent part of our lives in the CTC Western Division near the beginning of each new crop year, which always began on the first day of August in each calendar year.

Since the *WGTA* only allowed the Commission sixty days to process a complaint, these cases were invariably dealt with through written procedures and without any oral hearings. The specific issue in each case was a matter of law rather than of discretion in any event so written representations were an entirely appropriate method of dealing with them.

At that time, the policy focus shifted away from perpetually fixed rates for railway transportation. Furthermore, since public subsidies were now directly tied to the eligibility of a particular movement, any expansive interpretation that resulted in increased statutory rate eligibility could have an impact on the costs that had to be borne by both farmers and the government. These factors militated against an expansive approach to the interpretation of the new legislation and rendered interpretative rulings of the Commission after the enactment of the *WGTA* more conservative in their scope than pre-WGTA decisions.

The sweeping away of the historic *Crowsnest Pass Act* rates represented a significant change in policy approach by the government. By abolishing the old rate fixed by law since 1897, and replacing it with a new statutory rate that not only could be revised but one in which producers were expected to pay a significantly greater portion than they had in the past, the government had signaled its desire to move toward a modern and economically efficient system for the regulation of Canada's railways.

Several transitional problems requiring formal rulings faced the CTC Western Division in early 1984, as the new statute went into force. Those issues were largely concerned with the application of the statutory meaning of a "port in British Columbia" as it appeared in the *WGTA*. Problems arose as a result of the complex divisions of municipal jurisdiction in the greater Vancouver area. But those problems were quickly and easily resolved. Of more importance perhaps was a complaint by Alberta Food

Products and other canola shippers alleging that the initial tariff filed by the railways would require them to pay not only their own share of the freight rate but also the government's share of any deficit in respect of prescribed weight minimums on tank car loadings. That complaint was resolved in favour of the shippers and the offending provisions were ordered to be struck out of the railway tariffs. Later the CTC Western Division dealt with a variety of other cases such as complaints by alfalfa dehydrators concerning the application of the new rates to dehydrated feed pellets and cubes, railway positioning charges for marine containers, and the legality of diversion charges on statutory movements, as well as the eligibility of forage seeds in sacks for statutory rates. Generally, the CTC Western Division applied a principled approach to legislative interpretation and its decisions reflected a consciousness that efforts to squeeze other products into the eligibility criteria for the WGTA's subsidized freight rate were best left to Parliament and its delegate, the Governor General in Council, as those bodies had to bear the ultimate responsibility for policy decisions involving the expenditure of public funds.

The implementation of the *Western Grain Transportation Act* also had a significant organizational impact on the CTC Western Division. A new agency, the Grain Transportation Agency, was established in Winnipeg and it assumed responsibility for the coordination of grain car movements through grain ports covered by the Act. Our sub-regional offices and their personnel were devoted to this task in Vancouver and Thunder Bay, and they were transferred to the new agency.

Apart from the Crow rate cases, there was one other case during this period that dealt with some of the historic obligations of railway companies in the West. The case concerned the construction and operation of a new receiving and departure rail yard at Prince Rupert in British Columbia. In the early eighties the grain industry, in conjunction with the Province of Alberta, embarked upon a major project to build a new grain port at Ridley Island near Prince Rupert, B.C.. The intention in building this new grain port was to avoid the congestion that prevailed in Vancouver and to take advantage of the shorter hauling distance between northern grain delivery points and Pacific tidewater at Prince Rupert, which offered a shorter sea route to Asia.

The Canadian National Railway Company objected to a request by the proponents to construct and maintain at the railways' expense a new receiving and departure yard required by the project. This led to a complaint that the railway company was failing to fulfill its statutory obligations under the *Railway Act* to render the services that the public required. A hearing was duly convened in Prince Rupert in the spring of 1983 to hear the case of *Prince Rupert Grain Ltd. and Ridley Grain Ltd.* v *Canadian National Railway Company*[6]. For once it did not rain in this otherwise rain-drenched part of Canada.

Marshall Rothstein QC led the fight for the grain consortium while Canadian National was represented by Forrest Hume of its headquarters legal department in Montreal. The new grain port was a massive undertaking, designed to handle an annual throughput of 3,500,000 tonnes of grain with a monthly design throughput of 420,000 tonnes and a daily average of 19,000 tonnes. To support this magnitude of a throughput in the grain terminal a significant receiving and departure yard was required at an estimated cost of six million dollars.

In a sense, the grain terminal project was a fulfillment of the dream of the Grand Trunk Pacific to build a major railway terminus and ocean port at Prince Rupert. That dream had died with the bankruptcy of the Grand Trunk Pacific following World War One[7] and for decades thereafter the north line to Prince Rupert

---

6. CTC Western Division Decision: *Prince Rupert Grain Ltd. and Ridley Grain Ltd.* v *Canadian National Railway Company*, 1983.
7. The Grand Trunk Railway had also suffered a severe blow in 1912 when its President,

had languished as Canadian National routed most of its traffic to Vancouver over the main line that it had inherited from the Canadian Northern Railway Company.

At the hearing, the railway company admitted that a receiving and departure yard would be required and that it would be required at the location proposed by the grain consortium. The *Railway Act* provided that a railway company, as a common carrier, had an obligation to receive, carry, and deliver all traffic offered for carriage on the railway and to provide all reasonable facilities necessary for that purpose. The issue in this case was whether those obligations extended to a requirement that the railway company build and maintain a new yard and switch loaded and unloaded rail cars to and from that new yard. Although the issue was framed in terms of legal obligations an element of discretion was preserved in the statute due to the underlying standard of reasonableness which had developed in past jurisprudence and that had to be applied to any measurement of the railway company's performance under the *Railway Act*.

While the CN may have had an arguable point about the allocation of the costs of construction of the rail yard its refusal to provide switching services placed it in a difficult position since car switching is a service invariably provided by railway companies. In any event, the arguments, both legal and policy-based presented by Marshall Rothstein carried the day and were sufficient to persuade the Commission that the movement of western grain required the construction of the receiving and departure yard. The CTC Western Division granted the application and ordered Canadian National to construct and maintain the receiving and departure yard and to provide the necessary switching services. The railway company appealed this decision, first to the Commission's Review Committee in Hull, Quebec, and later to the

Charles M. Hays, lost his life in the sinking of the luxury passenger ship *R.M.S. Titanic*.

Federal Court of Appeal and then ultimately to the Supreme Court of Canada. It was unsuccessful everywhere.

Nevertheless, in their zeal to put the new grain terminal into operation on Ridley Island, the proponents decided that they could not wait for Canadian National to exercise its appeal remedies before construction of the facilities was undertaken. Therefore, they proceeded to physically construct the rail yard on their own according to the designs that the Commission had approved in its decision. Thereafter, the grain consortium and the railway company perennially argued over whether the railway company had been absolved of its responsibility to bear the cost of construction by the decision of the consortium to build the yard themselves notwithstanding the existence of an order from the CTC Western Division. However, the railway company did discharge its obligations under the original order to maintain the facility, and to provide a switching service in respect of the rail cars[8].

Much of the Commission's approach to this case had its antecedents in the nineteenth-century railway law of both Great Britain and the United States. The decision also reflected the perspective of the railways as an instrument of public policy in the old nation-building sense, and the continued validity of the obligations of a railway company under the scope of a statute that was virtually unchanged in substance since the nineteenth century. However, it was also apparent that the obligations which the railways laboured under had arisen during the nation-building phase of Canada's development and at a time when there were no other effective competing modes of transport. The retention of these obligations into the latter part of the twentieth century raised serious questions about the efficacy of the antiquated *Railway Act* and the policies that it represented in the modern context. As the century wore on pressure would

---

8. Operations began at the new grain-handling facility on March 11, 1985.

increase to review the legal framework under which the business of running a railway was conducted in Canada.

CHAPTER 7.

THE VARIABLE RATE BATTLES

From the beginning of the Crow Rate in 1897 the freight rates for grain transportation were based on the distance of each prairie delivery point from the great ports at the Lakehead in the east, or from Vancouver in the west. This distance scale existed irrespective of the cost of operating trains to any particular delivery point, although in theory the further away a delivery point was from a port the greater the cost of providing the rail service. For various operational reasons, this was not necessarily so but the distance scale did at least provide generations of western grain producers with a degree of certainty around their freight rates. That was widely welcomed because so many of the other costs faced by Prairie grain producers remained variable. The transportation cost of grain producers was therefore only a function of distance, which provided insufficient incentives for prairie farmers to agree to any rationalization of the western rail network devoted to the movement of grain.

To this locked-in scale of freight rates, there were two exceptions. The first exception allowed for contiguous or competitive rates. Contiguous rates allowed delivery points on adjacent lines of a single railway to bear the same rate. This prevented detrimental competition between the branch lines of a single railway. Competitive rates allowed one railway company to meet a lower rate offered by another railway company where the local circumstances would have led to a loss in traffic at a particular delivery point if the distance scale was applied. Competitive or contiguous rates had no positive impact on the efficiency of the system.

Rather, they tended to promote the status quo. Before the enactment of the *Western Grain Transportation Act*, the railways could utilize contiguous or competitive rates where it seemed necessary to do so. However, the new Act froze the existing contiguous and competitive rates and allowed no further contiguous or competitive rates to be offered.

The *Western Grain Transportation Act* contained one new feature that would have a substantial impact on the question of western freight rates and rail rationalization. The new feature was a mechanism to allow for variable freight rates. A variable rate was a freight rate that departed from the distance scale based on the volumes of grain delivered to particular elevator locations. The benefits of such a mechanism were obvious. Variable rates could greatly assist the railways and elevator companies in the rationalization of the grain handling and transportation system by identifying those locations that had a long-term potential as a grain delivery point, while conversely underscoring the limited future of the uneconomic locations. Producers could also benefit from the fact that variable rates would provide an economic incentive for their farming operations. By taking their grain by road to a point further away than their normal delivery points to take advantage of a variable freight rate some producers could end up with more money in their pockets. Clearly, variable freight rates could become a potent mechanism to accelerate the rationalization of the grain transportation system in western Canada.

However, due to the sensitivity of changing the historic distance scale for grain movements Parliament put two restrictions on the use by the railways of variable freight rates. The first and most important of the restrictions on variable rates was the need for a railway company to obtain the Commission's authorization for any variable rates. The railway companies would not be allowed to offer variable rates without government oversight. Secondly, a special restriction was put in place for the initial two years of operation of the new *Western Grain Transportation Act*. Any variable freight rate offered during that initial two-year period had to pass a special test set out in the legislation that required a railway company to show to the satisfaction of the Commission that efficiencies would be gained by offering a variable freight rate for the movement of grain. After the second crop year following the enactment of the legislation, this special test would no longer apply.

During the first crop year following the enactment of the WGTA, neither of Canada's two major railways attempted to offer a variable freight rate. However, in 1985, in preparation for the 1985-86 crop year, Canadian National applied to the Commission for permission to offer variable freight rates at certain locations on its lines where elevator facilities were maintained by Cargill Inc. and Pioneer Grain Co. Ltd.

The stage was now set for the 1985 variable freight rate battle. On the one side was Canadian National and two of the corporate elevator companies, including the American giant Cargill Inc. On the other side were the three producer pools, Manitoba Pool, Saskatchewan Pool, and Alberta Pool, all cooperative associations, as well as the Manitoba and Saskatchewan governments and a collection of non-governmental organizations concerned with rural life in the west. These groups were all adamantly opposed to the rail rationalization that the introduction of variable freight rates threatened to accomplish. Public interest in this case was intense and the media followed the debate closely. During the hearing reports about the case were featured on the nightly CBC television news program, *The National*.

CTC Western Division Commissioners McDonough and Wolfe proceeded with the hearings. The 1985 variable rates case, and the subsequent 1987 hearings, were the most contentious regulatory hearings that I participated in as counsel to the Commission. The 1985 hearings were particularly strained by bitter public opposition to the proposal on the part of some of the participants. The case for the applicants was led by Grant Nerbas as counsel for CN. He was assisted by an associate from the railway's Montreal headquarters, Terrance Hall, and on the other side was Marshall Rothstein QC, acting for the Alberta Wheat Pool, together with Jim Foran QC of the same firm who acted for the Saskatchewan Wheat Pool. Marc Monnin from their firm assisted both of them.

Due to the importance of the issue, it was decided that public hearings into the proposal should occur in all three Prairie Provinces. The hearings began in Winnipeg on Monday, March 4, 1985, where they lasted for only one day. On Thursday, March 7 the hearings moved to Calgary, again lasting only a single day. As expected, public opinion in both provinces was against the proposal. The opponents had held their fire until the hearing reconvened in Saskatoon. Now, on Monday, March 11, the hearings got underway in earnest in Saskatoon. CN, Cargill, and Pioneer no doubt knew that their proposal was controversial but they may have been caught off-guard by the determination of the opposition to the proposal. At Saskatoon, Messrs. Rothstein and Foran pressed home swift attacks in their cross-examination of the proponent's witnesses. Both were highly capable senior counsel who had a wealth of transportation law experience between them. They quickly focused on the special test of system efficiencies that Parliament had mandated would apply during the first two years of operation of the *Western Grain Transportation Act*.

Canadian National attempted to deal with the efficiency question in a generic way. At a very basic level, Canadian National was asking the Commission and the participants at the hearing to trust its judgment that system efficiency would be gained through its variable freight rate proposal. Messrs. Rothstein and Foran, joined by other interveners, insisted that Canadian National provide its unit cost data to support the claims that efficiencies would be gained from the variable freight rate proposal. The opponents made a motion seeking an order from the commissioners to require Canadian National to provide its unit cost data to the commissioners and the interveners, and that the witnesses for the railway be subject to cross-examination by the opponents on the whole question of future efficiencies. Canadian National naturally opposed that motion and the CTC Western Division commissioners were called upon to make a ruling.

Unit costs were very sensitive data which all of the railway companies were loathe disclosing for commercial reasons. Although the Commission itself had access to unit cost data as part of its branch line subsidy program, such information had never been made available to the public. Parliament had even made it an offence under the *Railway Act* for any employee of the Commission to disclose railway unit costs, which served to underscore its commercial value. Ordinarily, it might be expected that any request by an intervener for an order requiring a railway company to disclose its unit costs would be summarily denied by the Commission. However, this was an exceptional situation, in which many of the participants believed that the way of life experienced by Prairie residents would be negatively impacted by a decision to approve variable rates. The commissioners briefly adjourned the hearing while they deliberated on their decision.

After reconvening the hearing the commissioners, in an exceptional ruling, ordered the railway to disclose those unit costs which would support its claims of efficiencies resulting from the variable freight rate proposal. When this ruling was read from the bench Grant Nerbas immediately rose to ask for an adjournment so that he could consult with the railway's headquarters in Montreal. When the hearing reconvened a second time Nerbas rose to advise the Commission that the variable freight rate proposal was being withdrawn, as the Canadian National was simply not prepared to release such sensitive information. This news stunned the hearing, as the effect of withdrawing the proposal was to terminate the proceeding.

Later that night I listened as Knowlton Nash, newscaster on CBC's television's, *The National*, explained to the country that western freight rate case which had been thought to foreshadow major changes on Prairies had suddenly, and unexpectedly, ended with the surprise withdrawal of the variable rate proposal.

Some observers were disappointed with this outcome, as they thought that an incentive basis for rail rationalization would separate the economics of rail rationalization from its politics. However, a better view was that the law worked the way Parliament had intended it to work. Parliament did not want variable freight rates to be created unless the railways could prove that efficiencies would result during the two years following passage of the legislation, as Parliament was aware that the new Act would create a series of far-reaching changes during that period. In the longer term, the early success of the opponents in stopping variable freight rates from being implemented so soon after the enactment of the WGTA gave legitimacy to the process by which they were ultimately approved.

In 1986, neither of the major railways was interested in re-engaging on the variable rates battlefront. However, Canadian National did file a small proposal to offer a reduced rate at Dawson Creek, British Columbia, and Pouce Coupé, Alberta, to meet the competition that was being offered by the British Columbia Railway. Paradoxically, Cargill Grain Inc. applied for leave to appeal that rate on the grounds that Canadian National had not offered to enter into a general variable rate proposal with it in respect of the 1986-87 crop year, as it had done previously (and unsuccessfully) in the 1985-86 crop year. The Commission dismissed Cargill's application for leave to appeal and the CN's minor variable rate was put into effect for that crop year.

The main battle was renewed in 1987, in respect of the 1987-88 crop year. By that time the special transitional rule requiring proof of efficiencies had expired. Once again Canadian National, represented by Grant Nerbas, took the lead in seeking variable freight rates. This time not only the Cargill and Pioneer Grain companies supported the proposal, as in 1985, but the CN also had the backing of the farmer-owned United Grain Growers, as well as three smaller grain companies, Northern Sales Co. Ltd., Alberta Terminals Ltd., and Stow Seed Processors Ltd. Canadian National offered a reduction of $1.50 per tonne in respect of grain loaded into strings of 18 hopper cars during one 24-hour period provided that the grain was consigned to a single destination and that the receiving grain elevator was located on a rail line with a gross maximum rail car weight standard of 250,000 lbs. (113,400 kg).

As in the past, a wide diversity of prairie opinion was mobilized against this proposal. Chief among the opponents to the proposal were the government of Manitoba and the government of Saskatchewan, together with the Saskatchewan Wheat Pool, the National Farmers Union, and a disparate group of public interest groups, municipalities, religious orders, and individuals. The chief luminaries amongst the opponents included the Hon. John Plohman, the Manitoba Minister of Highways and Transportation, and the Hon. Emmett Hall, the former Justice of the Supreme Court of Canada who appeared on behalf of the Family Farm Foundation. The Aikins MacAulay and Thorvaldson law firm was once again present in the persons of Jim Foran QC and Marc Monnin, who represented the Saskatchewan Wheat Pool.

Neither the Alberta Wheat Pool nor the Manitoba Wheat Pool participated and the Government of Alberta intervened in the process this time in support of the proposal. Those differences illustrated the perceptual changes that were underway in the West concerning the grain handling and transportation system. Nevertheless, the variable rate proposal remained hotly contested across the three Prairie provinces, though public views were not quite as bitter as they had been in 1985.

The hearings before the Commission's Railway Transport Committee began in Winnipeg on Monday, March 23, 1987, and continued in Regina on March 24 and 25th before transferring to Saskatoon on March 26 and 27 and finally terminating in Edmonton on Monday, March 30. The quorum consisted of Commissioner Bernie Wolfe from the CTC Western Division together with two commissioners from CTC headquarters in Hull, Quebec, Commissioner Marcel Lambert PC, QC, a former Speaker of the House of Commons and a former Progressive Conservative MP from Edmonton, and Paul Langlois, a former Liberal MP from Chicoutimi, Quebec, who presided as Chairman. I participated as the legal counsel to this hearing panel.

The issue for decision was put to the Commission at the outset of the hearings in Winnipeg by the chief witness for the Province of Manitoba, the Hon. John Plohman, Minister of Highways and Transportation. He stated that the Government of Manitoba supported lower freight rates for all grain producers. However, the current proposal only applied to certain select centres and, as such, was very discriminatory. The Province of Manitoba, he went on to say, had always been on record as opposing variable rates believing that over the longer term, the introduction of incentive or lower rates at major delivery centres would lead to a diversion of grains to the highway for longer hauls, the closure of elevators, and the abandonment of railway branch lines.

Plohman contended that loss of elevator and rail taxes along with increased road costs due to heavier traffic would result in higher costs to municipalities. That, in turn, would be passed on to municipal taxpayers. Business activity would be curtailed and rural communities would decline. That would not be in the public interest.

A key element of Manitoba's position was that variable freight rates would lead to accelerated rationalization and a resulting increase in highway traffic would effectively download substantial infrastructure costs from an area of federal responsibility (railways) to a provincial field of responsibility (highways). Opponents of branch line abandonment throughout the rail rationalization era had repeatedly raised that argument.

The Province of Saskatchewan also opposed the proposal but not with the same stridency as Manitoba did. The main witness for Saskatchewan, the Hon. Grant Hodgins, Minister of Highways and Transportation, testified that while the province was opposed to variable freight rates it would support the extension of any approved reduction to all points in Saskatchewan that were capable of meeting the CN's criteria, including points on the lines of Canadian Pacific. That was evidence of a shift in opinion by Saskatchewan from the 1985 variable freight rate case. The opposition Saskatchewan New Democratic Party also appeared and opposed the variable freight rate proposal. Its star witness, Mr. Eric Upshall MLA evinced no subtleties in the views of that opposition party on the issue.

The Alberta Wheat Pool gave tacit agreement to the variable freight rate proposal of 1987 by its decision not to take part in the proceeding. That position, together with the active support of the proposal by some Alberta-based grain industry participants, the province's more diversified agricultural economy (which included a large cattle industry), and the fact that Alberta produced more of the lower value grains such as barley may have induced the province of Alberta to intervene in support of the 1987 variable rate proposal. Alberta's support gave some wind to the 1987 CN proposal and was a far cry from the headwind gale of opposition that the CN had encountered in the 1985 case.

As the hearing progressed, the Commission heard a similar message in Winnipeg, Regina, and Saskatoon – that variable freight rates would be detrimental to the prairie way of life. Many distinguished persons and organizations including former Supreme Court Justice Emmett Hall and representatives of religious orders such as the Ursuline Sisters, and the members of St. Peter's Abbey, as well as provincial and local politicians, and individual farmers, all argued that view. Saskatchewan Wheat Pool insisted that it would not take advantage of variable freight rates even if the Commission were to exercise its power to extend any approved rates to additional points.

All of the variable rate opponents stressed the point that variable rates could destroy the socioeconomic fabric of prairie society. The Saskatchewan Urban Municipalities Association asserted that Canadian National had social obligations and could not be allowed to influence grain delivery patterns for commercial reasons. The National Farmers Union argued that the proposal would establish a detrimental precedent for rate discrimination without any savings to farmers or the grain handling and transportation system. The National Farmers Union also made an interesting legal argument to the effect that the Canadian Wheat Board was the legal shipper of Board grains and not individual farmers. According to the National Farmers Union, the correct application of the law meant that any freight rate reductions should accrue to the account of the Wheat Board and not to individual producers.

Opponents of variable freight rates worried about the loss of country elevators

The only major Western agricultural group to support the proposal was the Western Canadian Wheat Growers Association (WCWG) formerly the Palliser Wheat Growers Association. A maverick group that occasionally took a contrary position to that of other major western farm groups, the WCWG argued that variable rates would accelerate rail line rationalization and that would be a good thing for western producers. A few public interest witnesses also gave evidence that tended to support the proposed variable freight rates, notably Dr. Storey of the University of Saskatchewan, who testified that potentially more rationalization resulted from government planning exercises than could be expected from the market-based approach of variable freight rates.

Canadian National and the six grain companies participating in the 1987 variable freight rate proposal stressed that the reductions in the freight rates would be passed on and that producers, and not the Canadian Wheat Board, would benefit from the proposal by a reduction in their shipping rates. Witnesses for the grain companies included the Hon. Otto Lang PC, a former federal Minister of Transport, who was now an executive for Pioneer Grain, and Hugh Horner, a member of a well-known Alberta political family, who was then President of Alberta Terminals. Those grain companies that addressed the rationalization issue stressed that rail rationalization was caused by many complex factors and would continue regardless of whether the variable freight rate proposal received approval.

All told the commissioners heard from more than 150 witnesses in six hearing days, often sitting late hours to accommodate everyone who wished to be heard. The commissioners deliberated before rendering their decision on April 10, 1987. In their decision, the commissioners dismissed all of the appeals against variable freight rates for grain and allowed the variable rates to be implemented. The commissioners also decided to extend the variable rate proposal to all points in the four western provinces that were capable of meeting the conditions for the variable rate as set out by the proponents. The commissioners dismissed the legal point raised by the National Farmers Union concerning the Canadian Wheat Board on the ground that the *Western Grain Transportation Act* contained a special statutory definition of a shipper, and the evidence of Canadian National permitted the Commission to find as a matter of law that the elevator companies participating in the variable freight rate proposal were shippers within the meaning of that statute.

On the more crucial issue of socioeconomic impacts, the commissioners noted that the evidence they heard was "heartfelt and sincere." However, there was an absence of evidence of specific direct harm to communities resulting from variable freight rates. The commissioners noted that some specialized trucking incentives were already being offered, such as the mill-door premiums offered by flour mills and canola crushers for grain delivered directly to a prairie mill. The commissioners noted that such mill-door premiums had not appeared to prejudice any community. Furthermore, the commissioners found that community decline was a function of much larger economic and societal forces, stating:

> For the most part, the evidence presented was cast as a scenario of decline of the rural prairie should lower rates are allowed. Even considering the potential effects of lower rates however, there is in our view unsubstantial evidence to show a direct attribution between a potential for decline and the proposed lower rates, bearing in mind that larger economic forces have, in the post-war period, led to increasing urbanization throughout prairie Canada.[1]

The written decision disclosed that evidence of academic opinion, such as the testimony of Dr. Storey of the University of Saskatchewan, was found to be credible, as was evidence that the survival of small rural communities often depended more on a community's social infrastructure, and on its schools and community facilities, than on its economic infrastructure.

Surprisingly, there were no formal legal appeals from the decision to approve variable rates. Opposition to the rates had burned itself out during the extensive hearings held in 1985 and 1987. The variable freight rates for grain went into effect on August 1, 1987, thus ending ninety years of fixed, distance-

1. CTC Railway Transport Committee Decision: *Appeals Concerning Proposed Variable Freight Rates for Grain Proposed by the Canadian National Railway Company*, 1987.

related rates that were originally instituted as part of the *Crowsnest Pass Act* rates.

The decision concerning the 1987 variable freight rates was one of the most important decisions that I was involved in during this period. Two aspects of the decision were of critical importance. Firstly, it considerably diminished, from a regulatory perspective, the concept of the railways as entities that owed special public obligations to society. All of the arguments about the importance of the railways for the maintenance of rural society were heard and dismissed. That was a significant break with the past and its seeming acceptance by the lack of appeals illustrated how quickly old viewpoints were being replaced by new public policy perceptions. In 1989, when several applications for leave to appeal the ensuing year's variable freight rate proposal came forward and alleged the same socioeconomic grounds for appeal as in 1987, they were all dismissed without the holding of any formal hearings.

Secondly, the 1987 variable freight rate decision highlighted the role of the elevator companies in the rationalization of the grain handling and transportation system. The nature of variable freight rates required an agreement between the railways and the elevator companies and thus ensured transparency in the use of the variable freight rate mechanism for rail rationalization purposes. By enhancing transparency in this process it was apparent that all major actors in the grain handling and transportation system participated in the ongoing rail line rationalization process. This helped the railways, at least perceptually, since they were no longer solely cast in the role of a large corporation that was attempting to abandon a community.

The 1987 variable freight rate decision did not entirely eliminate the western public's social concerns from transportation policy. Nor did it eliminate the effects of politics on public policy, or on its implementation. However, it did begin to reshape public attitudes and allow the formation of a new perception about the grain handling and transportation system on the prairies.

In the years that followed the 1987 variable freight rates decision, the concept of a variable freight rate became part of the regulatory landscape in western Canada, creating no more than ordinary interest by the western public. Eventually, all of the producer pools would feel compelled to participate in them notwithstanding their earlier opposition. Both the Canadian National and the Canadian Pacific would offer incentive rates as a market-based inducement to ease the process of rationalizing the western rail transportation network.

I was involved in one final variable rate case as the Canadian Transport Commission was replaced by the National Transportation Agency. Late in 1987, the Commission had received notice of variable rate contracts entered into by both CN and CP with the grain industry. The Commission had directed that public notice of the agreements be given and the case was then assumed by the new National Transportation Agency under transitional rules specified in the federal *Interpretation Act*[2] when the Agency began to function on January 1, 1988. One of the applications for leave to appeal from the proposed variable rates was filed by the canola crushers. The crushers had entered into variable rate contracts with both railways but now objected to the fact that the railways had restricted those variable freight rates by the terms of their agreement to hopper cars, which limited the application of the variable rates to canola meal and thereby excluded canola oil, which could only be shipped in tank cars. Due to the importance of this issue to the crushers, the leave to appeal application was set down for an oral hearing in Winnipeg early in 1988, which I attended for the first time in my new capacity as the Agency's Chief of Dispute Resolution in western Canada.

2. Interpretation Act R.S.C., 1985, c. I-21

In this instance, the Agency built upon the principles established by the Commission in the preceding cases. Agreements for the reduction of rates to enhance system efficiencies were desirable unless there was substantial and compelling direct evidence of prejudice to third parties. In respect of the parties to variable freight contracts themselves, there could be little or no basis for an appeal in the absence of duress, or fraud. Basically, the crushers had negotiated an agreement with the railways after which they decided to ask the rail regulator to rewrite that contract after it had been signed. The Agency dismissed the crushers' leave to appeal application, stating:

> Where, as here, an agreement is reached by two parties, it is not appropriate for this Agency to entertain an appeal designed to vary an existing contract by the extension of the contract, at the request of one of those contracting parties, to other products moved in different types of rail equipment, which is the remedy sought by the Applicants. This is particularly appropriate under this statute since, in the absence of a lower rate contract, the railway companies are entitled to charge only a regulated freight rate determined by the cost of transportation, and thus no real question of monopoly or unfair advantage through captivity is present in any real or substantive sense.[3]

By deferring to the intent of the parties in entering into a contractual relationship and the negotiating process by which those contracts had been derived, the Agency highlighted the necessity of the shippers and the carriers to mutually collaborate on the implementation of incentive changes to the grain handling and transportation system in the west and to bear responsibility for the results.

---

3. National Transportation Agency of Canada Decision: *Appeals by Canola Crushers Concerning Proposed Variable Freight Rates for Grain Proposed by the Canadian National Railway Company and Canadian Pacific Limited*, 1988.

PART IV.

PASSENGER SERVICES AND NORTHERN ISSUES

CHAPTER 8.

INTO THE SUNSET

Traveling by train brought home the vastness of the country. Going west from Saskatoon I could spend a whole day watching the rolling expanse of the prairie and its small towns and hamlets pass by my window. At night in a darkened sleeping car roomette I would watch low clouds scud over rank after rank of the spruce and pine trees of the northern forest, unbroken by any obvious signs of civilization. The same vistas had greeted previous generations of Canadians traveling across the vast expanses of the west that had been made part of Canada by the coming of the railway.

Sometimes, I would ride up front in the engine[1]. Traveling in the head end was fascinating and allowed me to watch the railway in action. As we crossed the prairie I experienced train meets and saw-byes[2] and I looked on as we stood out into dark territory where train control was not yet performed by automatic signals. Rather, orders continued to be hooped up to the engineer at station stops in a century-old practice that would soon be consigned to history. The engine crews on the passenger runs were high seniority men, and they regaled me with tales about the days of steam which they had known well (and did not miss!).

---

1. As an officer of the CTC I had a special pass that allowed me to ride in the engines.
2. *Saw by* means any move through switches or through connecting switches that is necessitated by one train overtaking and passing another on single line track where a train is too long to fit within a siding. A meet occurs when two trains approach each other head to head on a single-track line with one of the trains moving onto a siding to allow the other train to pass by on the main track.

I rode up front coming down from the mountains onto the prairie through the Spiral Tunnels, traveling past the marred landscape from the completed Lake Louise grade reduction project for which Parks Canada had expressed much indignation at the Mount Macdonald tunnel case. I rode with the engine crews through northern Manitoba past sidings full of antique box cars and cattle cars awaiting passage to the scrappers and listened to an engine crew's story about the time that trappers in this remote area found their captured furs inexplicably stolen out of their traps and eaten. The mystery was solved one day when their train, the *Hudson Bay*, traveled around a bend and found a wolverine on the track. The animal's cunning at removing prey from traps did not extend to avoiding trains. Like many other animals, it ran in a straight line down the track away from the engine, never veering to right or left, in a forlorn hope of outrunning the train. But the trappers were happy to have their trap lines full once again.

The crews were invariably courteous, as they saw in me a representative of the federal government[3]. When I wasn't riding up front, I took in the amenities of the passenger cars. On many of the western runs the train consist would include a dining car, a dome car, and perhaps an observation car offering a panoramic view of the countryside. Privacy was available in the sleeping cars on the long-distance trains, where roomettes or bedrooms were available.

The train offered the opportunity for reflection, relaxation, and

---

3. Once I took a table in the the Dining Car of a Via train where a veteran employee was sitting. A young brakeman came up to the table and reported to the older employee that he had spoken to the conductor and learned that there was a "spotter" aboard. The conductor knew this because one of the tickets was issued to a pass holder. The older employee assured the younger man that he knew all of the railway company spotters and had seen none on the train. However, he said, "I don't know the spotters from the Board of Transport, and it was possible that one of them was aboard." Neither of them paid the slightest attention to me probably because I appeared to be too young to be a "spotter"!

good conversation with interesting people. It remained a civilized, even romantic way to travel – if you had the time to do it. Passenger services had been a fundamental part of the business of the railways in western Canada. However, by the eighties, they had long since lost their place as the dominant form of public transportation and the government was now wholly responsible for the passenger train service budget.

Only a few years had elapsed since Via Rail Canada Inc. had been established under the authority of an appropriation statute enacted in 1977 and had assumed responsibility from Canadian National and Canadian Pacific for the extensive network of passenger train services that still cris-crossed western Canada. The entire passenger train system was uneconomic, according to the standard measures of economic costing embodied by the CTC in its *Costing Order R-6313*. That was also true of passenger train services in other countries as well. Everywhere it seemed, passenger railways constituted a drain on the public purse. Unlike highway transport systems a railway passenger train was required to bear a share of the capital cost of their physical facilities as well as to bear the operational costs of the passenger train sets. The real test was one of utility and not cost – did a particular passenger train service provide appropriate value given the cost of the service?

The involvement of the CTC Western Division in passenger train discontinuance cases under the *Railway Act* was limited since most services were now essentially a matter of contracts between the Department of Transport and Via Rail Canada Inc. Nevertheless, two exceptional situations in Western Canada did require a series of regulatory reviews to resolve their ultimate status. Both situations involved isolated lines, one on an island but said to be part of the famed transcontinental railway that brought British Columbia into Confederation in 1871, and the other traveling through remote regions of northern Alberta. Both of these services would occupy a great deal of my attention throughout the decade.

The first passenger train case to land on my desk involved the Via Rail service operated over the Esquimalt and Nanaimo Railway Company, a subsidiary of Canadian Pacific, located on Vancouver Island. The E&N railway (and it was never called anything but the E&N by the inhabitants of the island, despite Canadian Pacific's ownership of the line) served the communities between the provincial capital of Victoria and the town of Courtenay located north of Nanaimo. The crux of the issue here was a question of constitutional law. Was the continuous operation of the E&N passenger train service a constitutional obligation of the Government of Canada to the Government of British Columbia under its historic position as an element of the original transcontinental railway system?

Although the issue of whether the passenger train should be discontinued involved much more than a narrow question of law, the constitutional issue that hung over the hearing was framed by the Terms of Union between Canada and British Columbia, which stated in its eleventh term:

> The Government of the Dominion undertake to secure the commencement simultaneously, within two years from the date of the Union, of the construction of a railway from the Pacific towards the Rocky Mountains, and from such point as may be selected, east of the Rocky Mountains, towards the Pacific, to connect the seaboard of British Columbia with the railway system of Canada; . . . [4]

The construction of the Pacific railway as a line of communication between what was then settled Canada in the 1870s and the far-off Pacific Province of British Columbia was an essential term of the union between British Columbia and Canada. The

---

4. *British Columbia Terms of Union* 34-35 Vict., c. 28 (U.K.)

Pacific railway undertaking was a vast and complicated project for a new Dominion populated by only three million people in 1867. Indeed, the United States of America had only achieved a transcontinental rail link across the wide expanse of that country in 1869, despite its considerably greater population and resources and its more fortunate geography, which made piercing America's western mountains so much easier than in Canada. Nevertheless, against every obstacle, Canada's national railway project was finished in 1885 and it became a lasting achievement for the country.

The Esquimalt and Nanaimo Railway Company was given the task of extending the new transcontinental railway to the provincial capital of Victoria on Vancouver Island, a task which it achieved in 1886. A regular island passenger train service to and from Victoria commenced on September 30, 1886, and continued with variations but without interruption. By the nineteen-eighties, the service was being provided by rail diesel cars (RDC), which were self-propelled passenger rail cars manufactured by the Budd Company in the United States. The Canadian Pacific exerted determined efforts through regulatory hearings held in 1969, 1974, and 1978 to obtain permission from the Commission to terminate the E&N passenger train service. Although the CP actually succeeded in obtaining a discontinuance order from the Commission in 1974, that order was subsequently reversed by the Review Committee of the Commission in 1978.

In 1983, the Commission set down the 1969 application for discontinuance for a mandatory five-year statutory review. By this time Via Rail had become the operator of the service and its lawyers had carriage of the discontinuance application. Canadian Pacific participated in the hearing and adhered to neutrality until its final argument when it once again called upon the Commission to discontinue the service. The Province of British Columbia was active in the 1983 proceedings, as it was in all of the prior reviews of the E&N service. The province took the position that the E&N railway was part of the transcontinental railway that was secured to British Columbia by the Terms of Union with Canada and therefore it could not be terminated in the absence of a constitutional amendment.

The 1983 hearings were held in Courtenay, Nanaimo, and Victoria, and were well attended. The Chairman of the Railway Transport Committee, Commissioner John Magee, presided and with him was Commissioner Ralph Azzie, a New Brunswicker and former private secretary to Prime Minister Louis St. Laurent, and Commissioner David H. Chapman, a former labour leader from Vancouver. As it was a Western case, I was given the task of providing legal counsel to the panel.

Vancouver Island held the E&N passenger RDC's in sentimental affection and there was no lack of those who sought to preserve it. Via Rail, as the current operator, did not oppose retention of the service and that removed a potential emotional edge from the hearings. Nevertheless, there were plenty of complaints about the quality of the service that was being provided by Via, and part of my task was to pursue those issues on behalf of the Commission and the public.

Public banners proclaimed the affection of Vancouver Island residents for the E&N Railway Service offered by Via Rail

The E&N service was provided at the extreme end of Via's system and it was isolated from the mainland trackage. It was only natural to expect that the isolation of the service would have cost implications. Via ran the service with two Budd company RDCs. Both were self-propelled units that carried passengers and their hand luggage but did not accommodate checked baggage. Essentially, they allowed overnight trips up or down the island, between Courtenay and Victoria. Though it had some utility as a means of intra-island transport the real potential of the service lay in the tourist business, as Victoria and the island presented a strong attraction for visitors from other parts of Canada and abroad.

In the early eighties the E&N carried more than forty thousand passengers each year and so there continued to be a substantial patronage of the service. Most of the traffic was carried in the summer months which clearly indicated that it was more in the nature of a tourist service than an intercity passenger train.

Via Rail's passenger service on the E&N Railway was provided by Rail Diesel Cars supplied by the Budd Company

After hearing all of the evidence the Commission decided to keep the service for several reasons including its current utility, uncertainties around the economic viability of the island bus service, and the prospects for an increase in passenger rail traffic if improvements were implemented by Via Rail in the future. Canadian Pacific's half-hearted attempt to persuade the committee to discontinue the service was rejected. In ordering that the service be retained the commissioners skirted the constitutional issues which the province was concerned about. The decision was issued orally from the bench as an interim decision on October 7, 1983, and that was followed up by a final decision and order issued on April 11, 1984.

The Commission listened carefully to the concerns expressed by the public about the quality of the service and it directed that some further studies take place concerning the scheduling and frequency of the service, the possibility of beginning the train at Courtenay, the possible extension of the service farther north to Port Alberni, as well as ancillary matters such as food and beverage services, stations buildings and facilities, and the promotion and advertising of the service.

This was not the end of the E&N saga for me however, as the CTC Western Division had also been deliberating on a complaint previously filed by the Vancouver Island E&N Steering Committee concerning the minimum passenger fare on the E&N service. When Via took over the E&N service in the late seventies it imposed its national fare structure on the service, causing the minimum one-way fare to rise to $4.00. This was perceived to be a hardship on island residents who used the service to ride short distances and an appeal was filed with the Commission under section 281 of the *Railway Act*. The CTC Western Division held a hearing in early 1981 and issued an interim decision requiring Via to maintain a $3.00 minimum fare for a period of one year and to report to the Commission on passenger ticket lifts during that period.

The expiration of the one-year period occurred during a time when the CTC Western Division was heavily engaged in branch line abandonment work and inevitably the one-year interim period stretched into two years. Based on the results of the one-year interim period report however, the CTC Western Division concluded that there had been an insignificant impact on traffic as a result of the rollback in the minimum fare during that interim period and the fare appeal was dismissed, thus allowing Via to restore the $4.00 minimum fare.

The Province, which had not hitherto involved itself in the fare proceeding now sought and obtained the right to present an application to the Commission's Review Committee in Hull, Quebec alleging that new facts had arisen which warranted a review of the CTC Western Division decision. The new facts consisted of more recent traffic figures and were submitted in an application for review filed by the Hon. Alex Fraser, Minster of Highways and Transportation. On March 21, 1985, the Review Committee decided that the CTC Western Division decision should be declared reviewable "on the ground that new facts (i.e., new rider-ship figures) have arisen since the date the Decision and Order issued."

Commissioner David H. Chapman was assigned to hear the review orally as a single Commissioner and to file a report with the Commission's Railway Transport Committee on the merits of the review. As the CTC Western Division counsel, I was requested to accompany him and act as his legal counsel during the hearing. The Province acted as the Applicant in the review, since the steering committee elected not to present any further evidence although it did participate in cross-examination. Furthermore, Via now raised its minimum fare to $5.00 causing two local political leaders, Ms. Barbara Wallace, M.L.A. Cowichan – Malahat, and Mr. James Manly M.P. Cowichan – Malahat – The Islands to take up cudgels and together they filed further applications under section 281 of the *Railway Act*, which were consolidated and dealt with as part of the review.

After hearing the evidence, Commissioner Chapman concluded that there had been an effective segmentation of the market for transportation services. Short-haul passengers took the bus service operated by Island Coach Lines while Via dominated the long-haul market between Victoria and Courtenay. Indeed, the evidence showed that two-thirds of the total passengers took the train during the summer months, which was a clear indication that the train was primarily serving a tourist market, rather than a commuter or intercity transport market. The Commissioner concluded that the decision of the CTC Western Division should be sustained and the applications filed by Ms. Wallace and Mr. Manly should be dismissed. A final order to that effect was issued on November 8, 1985.

Although that was the end of my role in E&N matters, it was by no means the end of the E&N saga. When the Commission was replaced by the National Transportation Agency at the beginning of 1988 there was a failure to hold a five-year review of the E&N service in 1989, as the *Railway Act* demanded. After the fifth anniversary of the continuation order the Governor in Council, acting under a provision of the *National Transportation Act 1987*, which gave it the legal power to vary any order or decision of the Agency, attempted to terminate the passenger service. That action was challenged in the courts by the Province which was successful in the British Columbia Supreme Court, before Chief Justice Esson. The Chief Justice found that while there was no express constitutional obligation on Canada to continuously operate the E&N service such an obligation could be inferred in respect to the portion of the line between Victoria and Nanaimo, although not in respect of the later extension north of Nanaimo. Further, the statutes pertaining to the settlement arrangements between British Columbia and Canada respecting the E&N railway were special acts that overrode the more general provisions of the *Railway Act*. Finally, the order of the Commission had expired on its fifth anniversary and therefore nothing was left for the Governor in Council to vary under the powers conferred on it by the *National Transportation Act 1987*.

The judgement of Chief Justice Esson was appealed to the British Columbia Court of Appeal, which generally agreed with him. The Court of Appeal found that the obligations that Canada had entered into with British Columbia in the 1880s were constitutional obligations and not mere commercial obligations. Furthermore, even if Canada could unilaterally terminate the train service, the settlement statute enacted by Parliament at the time of the negotiations with British Columbia was a special act that could only be nullified by the enactment of another special act and could not be vitiated by reliance on the general provisions of the *Railway Act*. Finally, the Court of Appeal agreed with the lower court that the Governor General in Council could not vary an order to continue service issued by the Commission more than five years after it was made.

The federal government took the issue to the Supreme Court of Canada which, by a majority of Justices, reversed the lower courts and held that there was no constitutional or other restraint on the ability of the federal authorities to terminate the service. Firstly, the high court held that Canada had only taken upon itself an obligation to construct the railway and not to continuously operate it. Secondly, an agreement known as the Dunsmuir Agreement, which did contain an obligation to continuously operate rail services over the line, and which was appended to a statute of Parliament, had not been assimilated into the federal Act so as to become a law, and therefore no special act existed that could override the powers conferred by the general provisions of the federal statute which allowed the federal government to discontinue the E&N passenger train service.

Finally, the Court said that the order issued by the Commission in 1984 was an order that had a continuing legal force notwithstanding the failure of the National Transportation Agency to conduct another five-year review. Thus, the Governor in Council did have the authority to vary the Commission's order to terminate the E&N passenger train service.

The result of this major constitutional battle between the federal and provincial authorities resulted in a clear victory for the national government. However, perhaps exhausted by these battles the federal authorities took no immediate action to terminate Via service on the line[5].

As the eighties progressed, serious rationalization of the western passenger rail network proceeded apace. Service was cut between Saskatoon and Prince Albert, Saskatchewan, and the *Super Continental*, a once famed CN transcontinental service, was cut and replaced by daily trains between Winnipeg and Saskatoon, and between Saskatoon and Edmonton. Later, those services were terminated and the *Super Continental* was restored, as a Winnipeg – Saskatoon – Edmonton – Vancouver service. Finally, the famed CP transcontinental train, the *Canadian* was terminated and the *Super Continental* service extended to Toronto, the whole being renamed the *Canadian*, although much of the new route had no historic connection to the CP service. This last revision left all points west of Winnipeg on the CP main line without transcontinental passenger rail services.

5.. Passenger train services on the E&N were eventually suspended in 2011 due to concerns about the track structure. The E&N railway itself was subsequently transferred to an island foundation by CP in 2006.

Via Rail's premier train, the Canadian, on CP trackage before the southerly route was terminated in favour of a new routing over northerly CN lines

Eventually, Via Rail transferred its passenger-train service between Vancouver and Calgary to a new company, which operated a train named the *Rocky Mountaineer*. That however, was not a true passenger train service but rather was a type of land cruise tour through the pristine beauty of the Rocky Mountains which did not entrain or detrain passengers along the way, or provide a regular scheduled passenger train service.

North and south services between Regina and Saskatoon and Calgary and Edmonton were also terminated. In the latter case, there had been worries about safety following a tragic accident in 1983 in which a CP work crew left a main line switch lined for a siding occupied by stationary tank cars at Wessex siding. When the passenger RDC unit came down from Edmonton on its way to Calgary, it hit the open switch and the engineer was unable to stop the RDC before it entered the siding and slammed into the tank cars. Five people, including the engineer, lost their lives. I served as a legal advisor at a subsequent Board of Investigation headed up by our Director of Rail Operations – Western Division, Martin Lacombe. The circumstances of the accident involved an omission on the part of the foreman of the work crew who did not remember to realign the switch after exiting the siding with the work train, with tragic consequences. A formal inquiry into this unfortunate accident was subsequently conducted by the Commission's Railway Transport Committee.

In British Columbia, I had been present in the front cab of the E&N RDC (Via's *Malahat*) unit viewing at first hand the crossing of the tracks by dump trucks and other vehicles over crossings without signals only a short distance ahead of our oncoming RDC unit as it traversed the E&N line between Courtenay and Parksville in British Columbia. That experience was a real eye-opener for me about the vulnerability of an RDC unit in a collision.

For a while there was a Manitoba proposal, keenly supported by Commissioner Bernie Wolfe in the CTC Western Division, to operate a railbus service in northern Manitoba as a supplement to the regularly scheduled Via train, the *Hudson Bay*. It was thought that the railbus could serve the transportation needs of the inhabitants of the reserves established under the *Indian Act*[6]. The project involved taking a regular bus and putting trucks on it (i.e., train wheels). CTC Western Division staff gave technical assistance to this project under Commissioner Wolfe's direction. Unfortunately, this physical configuration proved to be unstable and when the wheels fell off the prototype unit that was the end of the railbus experiment!

Toward the latter part of the eighties, I became preoccupied with another passenger rail case that had been left to the Commission in western Canada. A rather antique mixed train service was

---

6. . *Indian Act*, R.S.C.1985, c. I-5.

operated by Canadian National in northern Alberta between Edmonton and Waterways. A mixed train is a combined freight and passenger train. Canadian National had inherited this service from the Northern Alberta Railway which CN had acquired on January 1, 1981.

Such mixed trains were once common on more remote routes which did not warrant, or could not economically support, a dedicated passenger train service. The mixed train service in this case had originally been instituted by the predecessors of the Northern Alberta Railway on November 7, 1915.

This mixed train service, sometimes called the *Muskeg Flyer*, was one of the last two passenger trains operated by CN in Canada as all other CN services had been transferred to Via Rail. The passenger component of the mixed train consisted of a baggage/express car and a comboose (a combined passenger coach and caboose). Later in the decade, it would consist of one (sometimes two) coaches, a combined baggage/express car and a caboose tacked onto the CN scheduled freight trains between Edmonton and Waterways, which was the rail terminus for the northern Alberta oil sands boom town of Ft. McMurray.

The mixed train service was a link between isolated northern communities and the south. Many of the communities were landlocked in the sense that they lacked access to overland communication routes other than the railway. Groceries, goods, mail, newspapers, and carload freight traveled north from Edmonton, and furs, game, mail, grain, and minerals came south. Passengers consisted mostly of indigenous residents and trappers traveling between points in the seemingly interminable northern muskeg. During the warm summer months, the service also attracted rail fans from around North America and abroad who were eager to ride the antiquated service before it disappeared. Due to its isolated nature and the length of the 263-mile (423-kilometre) service the train crew offered their own coffee, soft drink, and sandwich service, and the conductor operated a cheque-cashing service for isolated residents along the line.

Canadian National incurred a loss in operating the service which prompted it to apply for discontinuance on October 3, 1983, on which date the CN became eligible for an uneconomic passenger-train subsidy under the *Railway Act*. The CTC Western Division began to examine the service earnestly in 1985. Upon initially inspecting the service, our Director of Rail Operations, G.G. (Bud) Ripley, promptly condemned the comboose car used on the route. The antiquated comboose was of World War I vintage and no longer met the current safety standards for passenger rail operations. Canadian National immediately withdrew the car from the service and delivered it to the local rail museum in Ft. McMurray, where I had an opportunity to tour it later in the year during the CTC Western Division's hearings into the passenger train discontinuance application.

At the passenger train discontinuance hearing the evidence showed that the service still provided the only means of transportation for ten isolated communities between Lac La Biche and Waterways. Due to the lack of an alternate, effective, method of transportation, the CTC Western Division decided that the passenger train service should be retained and accordingly it issued a decision requiring that CN continue to operate the *Muskeg Flyer*[7]. Given the lack of transport facilities in the area, even Canadian National did not object to retaining the service, at least until an ongoing road construction program by the Province eliminated the need for the passenger train service altogether.

The CTC Western Division also took this opportunity to examine the quality of the service being provided to the public and to compel changes in the public interest. Although the depression-era coach which replaced the comboose was found to be ade-

---

[7]. Decision WDR1986-01; January 28, 1986

quate, an additional coach was deemed to be required to protect the service in case of a mechanical failure on the first coach, and to deal with surge demands for carriage, particularly in the summer.

The CTC Western Division was alarmed at the practice of carrying overflow passengers in the baggage/express car. Commissioners and staff examined the car and determined that a hazard was presented by this practice. In a collision, passengers standing or sitting on the floor of the car could be crushed by the movement of heavy express shipments, or if the refrigeration equipment in the car broke away. Accordingly, the CTC Western Division prohibited this practice, relying on a ruling made in an early E&N discontinuance case, where a similar practice had been deprecated[8].

Anticipating the need for a second coach, Canadian National advised the Commission at the hearing that it had already purchased an old coach from Via Rail but that to place it into service would cost a breathtaking $600,000.00 in upgrading costs! Nevertheless, as the service required a second coach for the safety and comfort of the traveling public the CTC Western Division approved the cost, which had to be paid by the government through the subsidy provided for the uneconomic operation of the passenger train service.

Passenger shelters were in a deplorable state along the route, when they existed at all. The CTC Western Division directed CN to examine the condition of the shelters and to make any necessary improvements. Although the commissioners concurred with the view that freight operations on the mixed service took precedence the railway was encouraged to adhere to the passenger train schedule as closely as possible in order to accommodate passengers.

---

[8]. .Decision WDR1986-01 and Order No WDR1986-130 dated May 29, 1986

The CTC Western Division also discovered that household staples and groceries were carried as express shipments with a minimum $35.00 charge. Perceiving that practice to be a hardship to the residents in this isolated northern area of the province, the commissioners suggested that the railway allow the carriage of groceries as checked baggage (i.e., free if accompanied by passengers).

Later in 1986, the CTC Western Division received new reports concerning service changes by Canadian National. Due to economic fluctuations, the demand for the carriage of sulfur (a primary freight commodity) had declined significantly, prompting the CN to cancel one of the regularly scheduled freight runs to which the passenger cars had formerly been attached. However, since the frequency of the passenger train service was fixed by the Commission's *Passenger Train Service Order*, the railway had begun running a dedicated passenger train from Edmonton to Waterways on Mondays and the mixed train service later in the week. By changing the service configuration to include a dedicated passenger train, all of the operating costs of the dedicated service had to be borne by the government, and that increased the costs of the service significantly.

Bud Ripley, was once again dispatched to examine the service. His report was circulated to the parties of record at the previous discontinuance hearing and their comments, together with his report, formed the basis for a service review decision, issued as Decision WDR1986-11 on November 28, 1986. In that decision, the CTC Western Division acknowledged the decline in northern sulfur traffic which had precluded the operation of two mixed trains per week, and that the costs of operating one dedicated passenger train service in addition to one mixed train service was unsustainable given a railway estimate of 126 passengers per week. The CTC Western Division also noted that ongoing road building by the Province could have impacts on the long-term utility of the entire mixed train service. Accordingly, the commissioners decided to issue a public notice of their intention to reduce the frequency of the service to one mixed train per week.

The Province of Alberta also took this opportunity to complain that the cost of refurbishing a second coach to satisfy the previous ruling would amount to $587,317.00, an amount that the Province suggested was outrageous. However, the Commission's *Costing Order R-6313* had the legal status of a regulation and it allowed the railway to submit such a claim. Some other issues were canvassed in this formal service review. The CTC Western Division noted that the CN had improved the service schedule so that patrons could now take the train from the landlocked communities to Waterways, shop in adjacent Ft. McMurray, and return without having to spend the night in Ft. McMurray.

The Janvier Indian Band expressed concern about the lack of any extension of credit by the railway to patrons of the mixed train service which the Commission felt was a matter that should be left to the managerial discretion of the railway company. The Janvier Indian Band also requested that consideration be given to fare and express rate reductions of 50% to persons holding valid treaty cards but Canadian National opposed any reduction of revenues on the service and given its uneconomic nature it was not feasible for the commissioners to give favourable consideration to that request.

The grain elevator agents disliked the reduction of the scheduled freight service, which occurred when the decline in sulphur traffic eliminated the need for one of the two scheduled freight runs per week but the elevator companies were still in as good (if not a better position) than at other elevator locations. Nevertheless, the CTC Western Division asked CN to state why it should not be ordered to operate one scheduled freight as part of a mixed train service over this route.

The frequency review prompted requests for maintenance of a two-train weekly frequency and additional suggestions for improvement from people concerned with the future of the service. However, the CTC Western Division decided, in Decision No. WDR1987-03 of March 10, 1987, that the costs of operating a dedicated service were unwarranted in light of the traffic levels which averaged 125 persons per week and which varied considerably according to season. Accordingly, the service frequency was reduced to one train per week.

It was also decided that this service should be operated as a mixed train to reduce the impact on the public treasury and therefore the CN was ordered to operate the passenger service in conjunction with a scheduled freight service. The commissioners took this opportunity to describe the appropriate train configuration, which the commissioners said should consist of motive power (i.e., an engine), an assigned box car capable of carrying less than carload traffic including pressure vessels and hazardous commodities, other freight cars if required (e.g., cars for carrying grain), a baggage/express car, one passenger coach (two if demand surged) and a caboose. This service configuration and service frequency were to be maintained for a one-year period. The decision noted that road building south from Ft. McMurray to Conklin continued and that the area encompassed by the road would include the area of largest demand for passenger rail services.

This decision was the last in a series issued by the CTC Western Division (Commissioners McDonough, Wolfe, and Chapman forming the quorum) as the CTC was replaced by the National Transportation Agency at the end of 1987 and the Commission wound up its affairs and was terminated in March 1988.

As part of the new National Transportation Agency, Western Region, our office began reviewing the service again in late 1988. Bud Ripley had stayed on with us as a Rail Operations

Investigation Officer and he was dispatched to the area to look over the service once again. Road construction was proceeding quickly and the Province had opened a new all-weather road from Ft. McMurray as far south as Conklin. The formerly landlocked settlements of Anzac, Cheecham, Mile 24, Chard, and Conklin now had access to an alternative means of transport. A rough passage existed further south to Margie, Philomena, and Mile 146, which was capable of being traversed by all-wheel drive vehicles. It looked very much like the service would become redundant the following year.

In the spring of 1989, I traveled up to the area in company with Bud Ripley and our Regional Engineer, Henry Heinrichs. There was little doubt that the all-weather road created by the province would not have been acceptable to many southern residents in the province but northern residents were more accustomed to rougher roads. The opening of the road had cut heavily into the passenger traffic on the railway by reducing its ordinary traffic to a handful of passengers. There was no longer an economic justification to retain the mixed train passenger service.

In its final decision on this service, the National Transportation Agency deemed it prudent to keep the service through one last construction season, as adequate facilities might not be in place before 1990. Since a winter road existed south of Conklin each year, all things considered, it seemed appropriate to keep the passenger train service until October 31, 1989. That was the decision that the Agency Board took and on that date, the *Muskeg Flyer*, Canadian National's last passenger train in the west, rattled into the sunset.

CHAPTER 9.

THE NORTH

The western provinces were the primary focus of my practice in the eighties particularly since my practice had a strong focus on railways. However, my practice also involved northern issues and it was in that area where I dealt with some significant air transport issues. Early in my career with the CTC Western Division, I had the occasion to act as assistant counsel in major commercial air licensing hearings held in northern Manitoba and the Keewatin District of the old Northwest Territories[1].

As the eighties dawned, national air transportation policy continued to be based on the concept of slicing the market for air services into segments and distributing them to the most capable applicants. The economic forces of a free market had only a limited scope in the regulatory structure for which the CTC acted as the national aeronautical regulator. Air transport services were generally of two kinds; charter services for air travelers in which the entire capacity of the aircraft was rented, or unit toll services in which a price per unit, such as a passenger, was charged. The air transport market was divided into three tiers (four if one also included the small local charter services available in any community with a sizeable population).

At the apex of the regulatory pyramid perched the national carriers, Air Canada and Canadian Pacific Airlines, each of which operated transcontinental services as well as transborder and international routes. Air Canada was a Crown corporation with

---

1. The Keewatin District of the Northwest Territories is now part of the Territory of Nunavut, following the division of the Northwest Territories in 1999.

a legacy as a tool of government policy in the development of the domestic air transportation network. As such, it continued to be favoured in the awarding of routes, particularly domestic transcontinental routes, transborder routes to the USA, and international routes to Europe and the Middle East. CP Air ran scheduled services across Canada and particularly throughout the West, as well as services to South America and Oceania. Beneath these two major scheduled carriers was a second tier of regional carriers which were intended to serve the needs of particular regions over routes that Air Canada and CP Air did not relish serving. The country was carved up into zones with Eastern Provincial Airlines occupying the regional slot in Atlantic Canada, Nordair and Quebecair in Quebec and Ontario, Lambair in Manitoba, and Pacific Western Airlines in the remaining western provinces and territories. Beneath these regional carriers, there was a tier of tertiary or local carriers which in the west included Calm Air in Manitoba, Norcanair in Saskatchewan, Time Air in Alberta, Air BC in British Columbia, and Northwest Territorial in the north. Finally below those third-tier carriers there existed the smaller charter airline services together with specialty services and helicopter services.

In this heavily regulated market, all routes and services were tightly controlled by the framework of government policy. Airlines were not permitted to create new routes without regulatory approval. The market was further divided by restricting the use of particular aircraft by the weight of an aeroplane. Thus, permission was often required from the Commission to operate a heavier or lighter aircraft in a particular service configuration. In some cases, the actual model of an aeroplane was specified in a licence, and deviation from the approved model required the prior approval of the Commission.

Yet despite all attempts to manage the market through heavy regulation government could not prevent the occasional bankruptcy from occurring. In 1981, Lambair was petitioned into bankruptcy, leaving a void in air transportation services in Manitoba and the Keewatin District of the Northwest Territories. A major commercial air service licensing hearing ensued early in 1982, and I found myself serving as assistant counsel to one of the Air Transport Committee's aeronautical law specialists, Walter Fedoryk. The hearings were organized as a joint project of our headquarters in the National Capital Region and the CTC Western Division.

Many of the communities served by air carriers in northern Manitoba were populated by native peoples. I found that the native leaders who appeared at the Air Transport Committee hearings had a sincere concern for their communities and in conversations that I had with them during breaks in our hearings several expressed to me the hope that higher education, which became a reality for increasing numbers of aboriginal peoples during this era, would lead to enhanced economic and social development for their people in the future.

One group amongst our aboriginal population that was developing a new economic assertiveness in the eighties was the Inuit people of the far north. The Inuit peoples differed from other Aboriginals in that they had not previously signed land claims agreements with the Crown and owing to their nomadic traditions and the limited resources in the harsh climate of the Arctic they had not been relegated to reserves like their indigenous counterparts in the southern lands. Although they had suffered due to a policy of enforced urban settlement in the fifties which deprived them of their nomadic lifestyle, their culture retained a vibrancy that gave the Inuit people a collective confidence. Through the instrumentality of the Inuit Development Corporation, they began to invest in northern businesses. A key area for their investment strategy was air transportation since there were few roads in the Northwest Territories and the railway in the eastern Arctic ended at Churchill, Manitoba. There was sea lift capacity by barge from Churchill and some ocean transport into the Keewatin from Montreal but in the main, the people that lived in Keewatin were dependent upon air transportation. The Inuit Development Corporation created Nunasi Airlines to secure a commercial air service licence to serve Keewatin out of Churchill and following Lambair's bankruptcy it applied for waivers from the route protection provisions built into the licences of other carriers so that Nunasi could serve Rankin Inlet, Coral Harbour, Eskimo Point, and Baker Lake. At the hearing evidence on behalf of Nunasi was presented by one of the Inuit leaders, Tagak Curley, who testified that the Inuit people were dissatisfied with the quality of existing air services in Keewatin and were concerned about the instability of operators as shown by the bankruptcy of Lambair, and the possibility that a monopoly of air services could result. He said that the Inuit Development Corporation had tried without success to purchase an existing air carrier and now wished to develop its own commercial air service.

The difficulty that Nunasi and all prospective new entrants into an air service market faced was that a new entrant had no track history to fall back on in comparison to existing operators. In a highly regulated market, this presented a difficult and sometimes insurmountable obstacle to market entry, since regulators tended to be cautious in their decision-making concerning market entry. In the end, Nunasi failed to secure authority to enter the commercial aviation business. The former Lambair authorities were parceled out by the Air Transport Committee in a complex market segmentation effort designed to give the most capable existing operators room to provide the services that were deemed to be required. Naturally, the Inuit Development Corporation was very disappointed with this result.

The most successful applicant at this hearing was Ontario Central Airlines (OCA) which had historically operated air services in northern-western Ontario but which had moved into the northern Manitoba market substantially following Lambair's bankruptcy. OCA was controlled by Barney Lamm[2], a Minnesotan who had moved up to Canada after the Second World War and who had created a lucrative fishing lodge business. His Ball Lake Lodge attracted a considerable number of wealthy American fishers and he integrated his lodge services with his commercial air services. Mr. Lamm was a very likeable fellow and he became acquainted with some of our commissioners and staff. As he told it, the post-war era during which he had built up OCA and his lodge operation was a different era from the world of the eighties. Certainly, he felt that in the past society could be more trusting. One time, after a dinner in Winnipeg, Mr. Lamm told me he once owned a painting by the noted American western painter Frederic Remington that he had kept in his fishing lodge – even leaving it there unattended throughout the winter months when the lodge was closed and deserted. No one ever disturbed it. But he finally decided that it was not a good idea to leave the painting unattended throughout the winter in the isolated and deserted lodge after an American fisherman had come up to the lodge to fish and had promptly offered Mr. Lamm seventy-five thousand dollars on the spot for the painting!

At the Churchill hearing Barney Lamm publicly stated, in response to the evidence of Tagak Curley, that he would be open to negotiations with the Inuit Development Corporation for the purchase of the OCA by the Inuit if the timing and financial issues could be worked out satisfactorily. This possibility took away the sting of defeat from the Inuit Development Corporation and within a couple of years negotiations between the Inuit Development Corporation and OCA bore fruit. Ontario Central Airlines was acquired by the Inuit and renamed Nunasi Central Airlines. The Inuit now had an airline with the ability and capacity to serve Keewatin. Nunasi Central Airlines provided a foundation for the Inuit Development Corporation to play a stronger

2. Despite a similar surname, he was unrelated to the proprietors of the now-bankrupt Lambair.

role in northern transportation, and the company subsequently expanded into marine transportation by taking over the Northern Transportation Company, which provided the sea lift service along the east coast of Keewatin out of Churchill, Manitoba.

Nunasi, like its predecessor OCA, continued to fly DC-3 aircraft out of Churchill and Thompson, Manitoba. I flew on one of its vintage DC-3s out of Thompson to Churchill and I remember the green look on the face of a young court stenographer as the fifty-year-old plane lumbered down the runway and ambled up into the air. I also had the distinct sensation of being inside a bellows as the aeroplane took off! We could not fly above 10,000 feet since the aircraft was not pressurized and it seemed to waddle through the air but there is no question that the DC-3 was a very reliable aeroplane – perhaps the most reliable aeroplane in aviation history. It has an honoured place in the history of commercial aviation in northern Canada and elsewhere.

The author standing before a Nunasi Central DC-3 in northern Manitoba

The north had been opened up in the thirties and forties by courageous bush pilots whose fortitude in the face of the great challenges that northern aviation can pose was legendary. One night I had the opportunity to chat with one of those old-timer bush pilots in the rather prosaic setting of Via Rail's *Hudson Bay* train in northern Manitoba as I was traveling to a northern hearing. He related several stories to me about flying in the north with only one's wits as a guide. One story that I remember in particular involved a flight he made to the north carrying a generator in a plane that was equipped with floats. He ran into some mechanical trouble and had to land on a northern river to deal with it. While he corrected the problem, his plane was slowly floating down the river. By the time he finished his repairs, the aeroplane was getting uncomfortably close to a waterfall. He was worried that he would not have enough river space to lift off with the heavy generator on board and, to top it off, he had difficulties restarting the engine. Somehow he managed to get it going and took off with just enough room to spare. All in a day's work in the north, in those days!

Railways were also important to the north. Although the Hudson Bay line stopped at Churchill, the railway provided an economic way to ship goods to a point close to Keewatin. From Churchill, goods brought north by rail could be transhipped farther north into Keewatin on the barge service offered by the Northern Transportation Company. Churchill itself is part of the Arctic region even though it is well below the Arctic Circle. It is above the tree line so the landscape can be much starker than in the south and although I was never there during the right season, Churchill has become a well-known destination for polar bear watching. Beluga whales can be seen offshore and I once spied them from a great height in Hudson Bay as our chartered Beechcraft King-Air left Churchill after a hearing.

Churchill had very much a frontier flavour to it due to its isolation and that prompted the commissioners at the hearings on the Lambair bankruptcy to take advantage of a privilege they had of accessing one of the federal government's private fleet of railcars. At the time the government still maintained a fleet of well-appointed historic railway business cars for use by Ministers of the Crown. The Commission had secured the right to use the government fleet by giving up its own private railcar, the *Northwind*, as a government cost-saving measure. Commissioners were careful about their use of the private railcars but since Churchill was fairly limited in accommodations they brought one up for the hearing and stayed in it for the duration of the hearing. One evening they invited the staff to join them for dinner in the private rail car (it even came equipped with its own chef!). We joined them in car no. 5, one that was often favoured by Prime Minister Trudeau who liked to travel by train. This was the only occasion that I visited one of the government's private cars and it possessed a well-appointed though a little dated interior reminiscent of the 1950s. The five-course gourmet dinner that evening was a triumph for the chef and it was easy to imagine what private railcar travel had been like in the heyday of private rail transportation in the early years of the twentieth century[3].

Later in the decade, the CTC Western Division returned to Churchill for hearings as part of a northern station rationalization process commenced by the CN. There was still a strong need for passenger shelters along the Hudson Bay line since Via Rail maintained an important rail transportation service to Churchill. The Commission allowed the CN and Via to remove the existing stations conditional upon the provision of adequate passenger shelters along the line at station stops, including Churchill. Although the passenger train was important to northern tourism, especially in connection with polar bear watching, questions lingered over the Hudson Bay line concerning its economic viability, and the viability of Churchill as a major grain-handling port. Since it was located so far north the permafrost created huge maintenance issues for the railway, as the track was subject to substantial frost heaving. Furthermore, the shipping season was much shorter than at the other major grain ports located at Thunder Bay, Ontario, Prince Rupert, and Vancouver, British Columbia. The economic viability of the port of Churchill was always in jeopardy. However, the Commission was not the key player in issues concerning the viability of the port. The Canadian Wheat Board played a major role because of its administration of the block shipping system for grain movements by rail. Although it is doubtful that the wheat board found the use of Churchill to be efficient, political circumstances required that it make some deliveries for shipment at Churchill to keep the port functioning. Churchill remained important to Keewatin and Manitoba, as it constituted Manitoba's only blue-

---

3. In the late eighties the government sold off its fleet of private railcars as an economy measure.

water seaport, as well as being the major seaport for the transshipment of goods into Keewatin.

Rail played a role in the Western Arctic as well and by far the most well-known railway in the Western Arctic was the White Pass and Yukon Railway that serviced the Yukon Territory and Alaska. The historic narrow-gauge White Pass and Yukon Route is intertwined with the history of the Klondike gold rush of 1896-99 and it was a favourite of rail fans in North America and elsewhere. However, by 1982 the railway was facing severe economic dislocation following the closure of the zinc mine at Faro, Yukon. Ultimately there was insufficient traffic to justify keeping the railway in service without the revenues from the mine traffic. Like the southern railways, the White Pass and Yukon could no longer effectively compete with truck traffic. Therefore, the railway was shut down but not formally abandoned. It remained in a moribund state for a few years until the development of the Alaska cruise ship industry justified reopening part of the line from Skagway, Alaska, to Carcross, Yukon. Even in its moribund state, it continued to be a railway subject to the Commission's jurisdiction and from time to time over the years White Pass and Yukon files would continue to cross my desk.

From time to time CTC Western Division commissioners and staff held meetings with provincial officials to discuss the transportation challenges facing the western half of the country. Despite intentions, the CTC Western Division was never able to routinely interact with its territorial interlocutors in the north but after our transformation into the NTA Western Region, I made it a priority in my new capacity as the Agency's western Chief of Dispute Resolution to re-engage with the territories. In 1989, together with my colleague Shane Stevenson, Chief of Market Entry, I traveled up to the territorial capitals to hold talks with territorial officials. The rapid deregulation of air transport services following the coming into force of the *National Transportation Act 1987* created new possibilities in the Northwest

Territories, both in terms of new air services and more market-driven changes to established services. Tourism officials in Yellowknife expressed to us their general satisfaction with the way the new approaches to air transport regulation were unfolding.

Shane Stevenson, Chief of Market Entry and Analysis at the NTA Western Region

In the Yukon, we found concerns about surface transportation. The moribund state of the White Pass and Yukon put greater pressure on the road network and with it the likelihood of increased road maintenance costs payable by the territorial government. Even with the railway in operation, the Yukon has always faced the limitations inherent in its geography, since the seaport served by the White Pass and Yukon Railway is located at Skagway in Alaska, and therefore beyond the ability of Canadian governments to influence in terms of services or facilities. The future of the White Pass and Yukon Railway remains both then and to this day closely tied to the fortunes of the Alaska cruise ship industry.

Skagway, Alaska is the port served by the White Pass & Yukon railway

PART V.

MISCELLANEOUS CASES

CHAPTER 10.

ODDS AND ENDS

Although the bulk of my activities concerned the regulation of rail transport there were from time to time other matters that I had to deal with. From the start, a substantial portion of my regulatory practice, about 20% before 1988, concerned the licensing of commercial air services. Much of that work was procedural, by ensuring that natural justice was provided in our file hearings, which were non-oral proceedings. Occasionally, I would have to interpret the *Aeronautics Act*[1] or the *Air Carrier Regulations*[2] made under that Act. More substantively, I would sometimes have to review transactions such as a transfer or change of control of a commercial air service or review management agreements entered into by air carriers to ensure that such agreements did not constitute a disguised change of control of an air service.

About once or twice a year the CTC Western Division would hold a public hearing into a particular air licence application or a series of air licensing applications. At public hearings, the applicants would present evidence to show why the public convenience and necessity required the grant of a commercial air service licence, the grant of additional authorities under an existing commercial air licence, or approval from the Commission for a transfer or change of control of an existing air carrier. The interveners in such cases were usually other air carriers who filed contesting applications or who sought to block the applicant to maximize their own ability to dominate a particular market.

1. Aeronautics Act, R.S.C. 1985, c. A-2.
2. *Air Carrier Regulations* C.R.C., c. 118

Public interest evidence from ordinary citizens would be lined up by the applicant and by the interveners in written submissions or oral testimony to support their respective positions. In the end, the Commission would have to choose winners and losers based on the commissioner's own judgements and such technical analyses that their experts were able to provide to them. It was a regulatory process that sought to segment air transportation markets into finer and finer tranches and to parcel them out to a fair number of air carriers in each market. In that way, each would obtain a little economic benefit but if one of the participants failed there would be plenty of alternative carriers that could quickly move in to keep the system running.

The structure of air licensing regulation was complex and many felt that it was perhaps no longer required due to the maturation of the air transport industry in Canada. Eventually, outside forces calling for regulatory reform became so great that governments that had for so long sustained the public regulation of commercial air transport services began turning away from it, a process that accelerated after the election of the Progressive Conservative government of Brian Mulroney, in 1984. With the enactment of the *National Transportation Act 1987,* the greater part of the former regulatory regime for commercial air transport was swept away, and what remained were largely *pro-forma* requirements relating to the possession of insurance and airworthiness certificates. The withdrawal of heavy public regulation had little overall effect on the actual provision of air services to Canadians, although it did substantially impact pricing by leading towards more economical fares in certain segments of the overall air transport market.

The Commission also had a very small jurisdiction over pipelines. Although the oil and gas pipelines were regulated by the National Energy Board a class of pipelines known as commodity pipelines was regulated by the Commission, largely using the provisions of the *National Energy Board Act*[3]. A commodity pipeline carried solids, usually but not always mixed with a liquid, and so they were sometimes called slurry pipelines. There were a few small commodity pipelines in Canada[4] but no major lines, although there were one or two major lines in the United States. Nevertheless, there were hopes in some quarters that slurry pipelines could provide a competitive alternative to rail transport although in the end the capital costs of construction rendered such initiatives uneconomical. Due to the interest in slurry pipelines in the early eighties the Commission's Commodity Pipeline Transport Committee came to Saskatoon on one occasion to hold a formal committee meeting, the only one of the Commission's modal committees to do so in my years with the CTC Western Division. I attended the proceedings, which also involved a visit to the local facilities of the Saskatchewan Research Council, a provincial research institution that was heavily involved in assessing the economic and technical viability of slurry pipelines. The Alberta Department of Economic Development also produced a major report on slurry pipelines during this period.

The Potash Company of Saskatchewan, a provincial Crown corporation, was interested in slurry pipelines and they hosted a dinner for the committee which I attended. Unfortunately for our hosts, the dinner took place on the night of the 1982 general election in Saskatchewan and the government of Premier Allan Blakney which had campaigned on the hoped-for popularity of "Saskatchewan's Family of Crown Corporations" was decimated and went down to defeat. Many of the Potash executives were political affiliates of the Blakney Ministry and one or two of them kept darting away from the table to go to the bar to check

---

3. National Energy Board Act R.S.C., 1985, c. N-7

4. A small interprovincial commodity pipeline was built between Hull, Quebec, and Ottawa, Ontario by the E.B. Eddy Company in the eighties to carry steam from one side of the Ottawa River to the other side. This small commodity pipeline came under the jurisdiction of the Commission because it crossed a provincial boundary.

on the televised results and report back. As they went back and forth they conveyed more and more negative reports to their colleagues and the mood at the dinner table became glummer and glummer until finally it turned into a wake. The same could be said about the potential for slurry pipelines as alternatives to the railways. It was a prospect that never came to fruition due to the capital costs involved, and the competition that the railways provided. The Commission's jurisdiction over commodity pipelines languished. Later, in the mid-nineties, the National Transportation Agency's jurisdiction over commodity pipelines was transferred to the National Energy Board. It made more sense to place it there as an adjunct to that Board's knowledge and expertise with oil and gas pipelines.

Telegraph lines were another obscure area of the Commission's jurisdiction that crossed my desk. The Commission had been the nation's main regulator of telegraphs (a declining form of communication[5]) and telephones until 1977, when it was realized that it made more sense to vest jurisdiction in all forms of communication in the Canadian Radio-Television Commission which then became known as the Canadian Radio-television and Telecommunications Commission (CRTC). However, it turned out that one aspect of telephone and telegraph regulation concerning the height of the telegraph or telephone wires above railways, where the wires were owned by a railway, was not desired by the CRTC and it was subsequently transferred back to the CTC by the device of an Order-in-Council made under the *Public Service Rearrangement and Transfer of Duties Act*[6]. A dispute arose between the CN and certain rural municipalities in Alberta concerning the costs of telegraph line crossings and that required the CTC Western Division to investigate and determine the matter. That dispute was the subject of a formal decision that recon-

---

5. Surprisingly, it was still possible in 2012, when this work was originally published, to send a telegram in Canada through a firm called Telegrams Canada.
6. *Public Service Rearrangement and Transfer of Duties Act* R.S.C. 1985, c. P-34

firmed that the application of the senior and junior rule was appropriate in the case of wire crossings[7]. It was the final decision by the CTC respecting telegraph systems.

A large bulk of routine regulatory work that I had to deal with concerned the construction, maintenance, upgrading, and cost allocation of railway crossings involving municipalities and highway authorities in the western provinces and northern territories. The Commission's engineering staff in Winnipeg, Saskatoon, Calgary, and Vancouver were heavily involved in that work, and in the administration of subsidies under the *Railway Relocation and Crossing Act* for certain safety improvements at crossings. I worked closely with our Saskatoon-based engineers and our field engineers on such matters. Sometimes those files required an actual site visit to facilitate a resolution of matters in dispute between the parties. Occasionally, I also became involved with issues or disputes concerning statutory farm crossings created under the *Railway Act*, or private crossings established by agreement between a landowner and a railway. Such matters often necessitated some form of facilitation, or conciliation, to resolve the issues.

The CTC and the NTA exercised limited powers over marine transportation but that jurisdiction was exercised too intermittently to be delegated or deconcentrated to our western office as a program activity, or even in singular cases. However, our office did occasionally provide information to inhabitants of western Canada concerning the licensing of the northern inland barge services plying the Mackenzie River in the Northwest Territories, and on Lake Athabasca in Alberta and Saskatchewan. Our office also provided general information to Western Canadians

---

7. Decision WDR 1987-04, dated May 27, 1987. The senior and junior rule is a principle of railway law that apportions the cost of normal work to be performed at railway crossings. It states that the party whose infrastructure was put in place first should not have to bear the cost of work done at its point of intersection with the infrastructure of other parties. Those costs are to be borne by the other (junior) party.

on the *Shipping Conferences Exemption Act, 1987*[8], which permitted rate cartels for ocean transport.

The efficiency of Canadian ports was a significant concern to both the CTC and the NTA. Much work was done in a research capacity to determine the most efficient means of moving traffic, particularly grain traffic, through the west coast ports, as well as the Lakehead ports and the port of Churchill. But most of the time the work we did about ports was part and parcel of our work concerning the regulation of the railways, such as in the case of the Prince Rupert receiving and departure yard, and the rerouting of dangerous commodity traffic out of Coal Harbour in downtown Vancouver. There was also a proposal to develop an inland container port in Saskatoon that generated a service dispute between the proponents, the N. Yanke Trucking Company, and CN and CP which developed into a public hearing by the NTA in Saskatoon in the autumn of 1990. Ultimately, the Agency found that the railway was meeting all of its public obligations and the complaint was dismissed.

I did have occasion to hold discussions and meetings from time to time with officials of the Fraser River Port in the lower mainland of British Columbia. The port authority was concerned about the adequacy of its facilities and its competitive position vis-a-vis other ports in the lower BC mainland. Neither the CTC nor the NTA had much direct jurisdiction over the ports, however. The only specific power the CTC had was a very narrow jurisdiction under the *National Harbours Board Act*[9] to grant authority to established ports to acquire additional lands through expropriation, basically by using the provisions of the *Railway Act*. In the end, the federal government adopted the wise course of securing the amalgamation of all of the ports in the BC lower mainland which eliminated any element of port competition and

---

8. *Shipping Conferences Exemption Act*, 1987 R.S.C. 1985, c.17 (3rd Supp.)
9. *National Harbours Board Act* R.S.C. 1985, c. 10

allowed for the rational management of all of the available facilities.

One expropriation case that I did take part in during the eighties occurred entirely outside of western Canada. The Canadian Transit Company, the owner of the Ambassador Bridge linking Windsor, Ontario, to Detroit, Michigan, desired to expand the bridge plaza to support expanded customs and immigration facilities at the busiest border crossing between Canada and the United States. The Commission's General Counsel, Margaret Bloodworth, remembered that Windsor was my hometown, and she offered the case to me which I gladly accepted.

The Ambassador Bridge was built in 1929[10] and at the time of its construction it was the largest suspension bridge linking two countries in the world. The strong and steady growth in motor carrier transport throughout the mid-twentieth century resulted in greater and greater volumes of truck transport utilizing the bridge. The construction of Ontario Highway 401, a four-lane divided highway with limited access provided a speedy route through southwestern Ontario to the American auto industry centred in Michigan. Additionally, traffic into Michigan could avail itself of the excellent US interstate highway system with connections west to Chicago via I-94 and I-96 or south (and north) on I-75. The Ambassador Bridge was the focal point for those connections. Furthermore, with a free trade agreement with the United States in contemplation, there was an anticipation that future traffic volumes could increase dramatically. Among the constraints that the bridge faced were the cramped physical structures on the existing bridge plazas in both Canada and the USA. On the Canadian side, the Canadian half of the bridge operator (there were two companies, one Canadian and

---

10. According to a private statute; *The Canadian Transit Company Act* S.C. 1921, c. 57, which gave the bridge company the powers of a railway company under the *Railway Act*, which in turn permitted the expropriation of additional lands by the bridge company with the permission of the Commission.

one American company but both were under common ownership) sought to redevelop the bridge plaza to accommodate the surging growth of truck traffic. Evidence showed that total traffic (i.e., trucks and other vehicles combined) grew from 2.7 million in 1961 to 5.7 million in 1981 which was one million more than a 1963 estimate of traffic growth had projected. Moreover, truck traffic had grown from 11% of the total in 1961 to 25% of the total in 1986. None of that evidence came as a surprise to me since I had grown up in West Windsor and over the years I had seen the traffic increase along Huron Church Road, which led directly to the bridge.

The bridge was often congested and that led to significant traffic backups both on the bridge itself and on Huron Church Road. The bridge company needed to expand its customs inspection truck compound and create a more efficient bridge plaza layout. To achieve that objective, the bridge company had to acquire several houses that were then being used as commercial offices along the road which bordered the east side of the bridge plaza. By the mid-eighties, the bridge company had largely succeeded in that objective except for one house that was being used by a customs brokerage firm. That firm had refused to sell its property to the bridge company because of the dearth of alternative facilities in which to house a customs brokerage business close to the bridge plaza. Therefore, the bridge company sought expropriation and the Commission after hearing the evidence was faced with the difficult task of balancing the evident public interest in a more efficient bridge plaza with the substantial impact that would fall upon the operator of a small business if the expropriation was allowed to proceed. In the end, the commissioners decided that the impact on the brokerage business was disproportionate to the impact on the bridge operator, particularly since the bridge company could implement an interim redevelopment scheme for the bridge plaza that would improve its efficiency, if not to the maximum extent that would have occurred if the expropriation had been granted. The application of the bridge company was refused but some years later I saw that the customs brokerage facility was gone and its lands were being used in the redevelopment of the bridge plaza. Perhaps the bridge operator sweetened its original offer for the lands.

Our liaison activities with the public and other levels of government continued to be important. Sometimes there were special functions as was the case in 1991 when Saskatchewan hosted a reception for the Canadian and American negotiation teams that were negotiating a new transborder air services agreement between Canada and the United States. I represented the NTA, as I was then serving as its A/Regional Director in western Canada (following the retirement of our Regional Director, John Kimpinski) together with my colleague Shane Stevenson, our Chief of Market Entry and Analysis, at a reception hosted by the Province at Old Government House in Regina, a magnificent and historic structure from which the Lieutenant Governors of the original Northwest Territories (the old Rupert's Land territory of the Hudson's Bay Company) had once ruled a vast domain in the nineteenth and early twentieth centuries.

The Province of Alberta invited us to inspect a new railway line that it had constructed to serve a new Daishowa pulp and paper mill in 1990. We inspected the line by hi-line rail car with our former CTC Western Division director of engineering Jim Cant, who was by then a private consultant with Stanley Associates, an engineering consultancy. We saw first-hand the difficulties posed by the unstable terrain. The line ran through hilly and shifting terrain and it was necessary to apply shotcrete quite liberally along the right of way to prevent mounds of Earth along railway cuts from moving too close to the track.

Sometimes we lent our expertise to the public where public safety was an issue. For example, in the cattle baron country of southern Alberta, we assisted the owner of a gas plant near

Pincher Creek whose private rail spur crossed a road and who was concerned about the risks posed by the intersection of vehicular and rail traffic in proximity to his gas plant. Our staff were able to provide recommendations for improvements to public safety at the crossing and to reduce the potential for liability. Later we lunched at the plant owner's comfortable ranch house, which sheltered in a shallow valley, following which we took advantage of the opportunity to tour his vast cattle ranch. At 49 square miles, nestled under the looming Rocky Mountains, it was larger than some small European countries!

Among the most satisfying engagements that I had with members of the public during my years in Saskatoon occurred in connection with my responsibilities for promoting the resolution of travel disputes that arose between passengers and airlines in western Canada. We started a regional ombuds service between airline passengers and air carriers as a subset of a larger national program coordinated out of our Agency headquarters in Hull, Quebec. Many times my colleague Wendy Kennedy and I would get calls or letters from passengers who had a grievance against an airline and we would help them to resolve it using our good offices with the airlines and by applying alternative dispute resolution approaches to problem solving. Many of the issues in the eighties and early nineties involved flight cancellations or sudden schedule changes which caught many people off-guard. As the airline industry moved into a new and largely deregulated operating environment there was a need for adjustments both in the commitment to service by the airlines and in respect to the expectations of passengers. We helped both to deal with the relationship fallouts that occurred during this time of transition.

In most of the incidents, the aggrieved passengers merely wanted some form of recognition from the airline that they had been inconvenienced, and an apology or a promise that the company would take steps to ensure that the incident would not be repeated. In some instances, if the passenger suffered out-ofpocket expenses, they sought reimbursement. I developed good working relations with airline consumer affairs personnel at Calgary-based Canadian Airlines and Air Canada in Montreal. I also dealt with a slew of foreign carriers, usually through their main offices in western Canada which were typically located in Vancouver. As well, we dealt with many of the smaller carriers across the west and north. Apart from some very general level coordination of efforts with our headquarters operations in Hull, Quebec, we were generally left to our own efforts and creativity in resolving disputes. That we were often successful was shown by the many letters of thanks we received from passengers.

My general approach was to look at what was reasonable in the circumstances. Most of the time the airlines offered regrets to the passenger and provided them with vouchers that would reduce the cost of purchasing tickets for future travel with that airline. In the case of damaged or lost luggage compensation had to be offered that was consistent with the public tariffs of the carrier, and sometimes more was offered by an airline to maintain a good reputation with its customers. There was almost always a reasonable solution to the disputes that occurred.

One case left an indelible impression on my memory. It was the case of the seal that got a seat! Late one afternoon I received a telephone call from a man who had experienced a distressing trip along the coast of British Columbia. He had booked two seats, one for himself, and one for his young son but when the pair boarded the aeroplane the man discovered that his son's seat had been taken by a seal that was being shipped south[11]. Since there were no other seats available, his young son was forced to sit on the man's lap through the entire trip (although perhaps the boy was thrilled to have a seal as a seatmate.) Naturally, the man was upset that a seat he had reserved for his son, and paid for, had been taken by a seal. He had been unsuccessful in obtain-

---

11. The seal was inside a crate.

ing satisfaction from the local officials of the airline but when we became involved the matter was resolved to his satisfaction. As part of the resolution, the management of the airline promised us that steps would be taken to ensure that such incidents never happened again[12]. The passenger was grateful for the result. I have often thought of this case when I reflect on the strange experiences that can befall people when they travel.

---

12. The commitment to avoid any future such incidents was important to the Agency since this particular incident had safety implications, as safety rules required that children over the age of two years be seated in their own seat, and that they wear a seat restraining device.

PART VI.

CLOSING ARGUMENTS

CHAPTER 11.

A WIDER VIEW

While the CTC Western Division was grappling with the issues surrounding the significant changes occurring to the grain handling and transportation system in the West, bigger things were happening at a countrywide and worldwide level. In the English-speaking countries the advent to power of Margaret Thatcher in Great Britain, Ronald Reagan in the United States, and Brian Mulroney in Canada had ushered in an era of market capitalism and deregulation. Everywhere, it seemed, academics and media pundits were extolling the virtues of deregulated markets and deregulation was the prescription of the day for economic growth in the transport sector. Particularly at air transport hearings, the Commission would hear from professors of economics who would speak to the Commission about the benefits of competition in air service markets. Our Senior Economist, Roy Proctor, who was knowledgeable in air transportation economics explained to me that the inconvenience of service interruptions notwithstanding, aeroplanes had inherent value and if economic turbulence resulted in air carrier bankruptcies it would still be possible for the economy to redeploy the air carrier's main underlying asset, which was the aeroplanes themselves. As the decade progressed the opinions of more and more people coalesced around the idea that some form of transport deregulation was required

With the coming into force of the *National Transportation Act 1987* Canada began its experiment with deregulation, following the path blazed by the United States which had previously abolished its Civil Aeronautics Board and most forms of market entry regulation in air transport services a few years before. It was interesting to see the reactions and consequences of the Canadian air transport industry to deregulation. Air Canada fought against deregulation of course, as it had been a prime beneficiary of the regulated environment. Nevertheless, following deregulation, it moved quickly to maintain its dominance of the Canadian market, an effort in which it has largely been successful notwithstanding a period of insolvency necessitating protection from its creditors in the early 21st century. The ability of Air Canada to capitalize on deregulation was strengthened by the government's decision to privatize the airline. As a private sector entity, it was no longer subject to public policy constraints as it had been when it was a Crown corporation. However, many of the private sector entrepreneurs and operators who one might have expected to embrace deregulation found the new market-driven environment not to their liking. The success they had achieved had been largely due to their mastering of the intricacies of a regulated market. Many decided to leave the industry or were compelled to do so by circumstances.

Thus, Canadian Pacific Limited sold its airline, CP Air, which was the nation's second-largest airline to Pacific Western Airlines which then renamed itself Canadian Airlines International. Canada's largest charter carrier Wardair transformed itself into a scheduled carrier and after its head-to-head competition with both Air Canada and Canadian Airlines threatened to destroy all three of them Canadian Airlines International bought Wardair at a premium. Unfortunately, the resulting debt burden proved too much for Canadian to sustain and it eventually went bust and was itself sold to Air Canada. Among the smaller regional companies Time Air, which served Alberta and BC linked up with Canadian Airlines International and then disappeared along with its parent into Air Canada while Nordair and Quebecair had previously been absorbed by CP Air before it was merged into Canadian Airlines International. On the east coast, Eastern Provincial Airways had also previously been absorbed by CP Air.

Among the local carriers Hi-Line Airways in Saskatoon grew by taking over Norcanair but competition proved ruinous in the end and Norcanair merged with Time Air, which then became part of Canadian Regional Airlines before Canadian Airlines failed and all of it was merged with Air Canada. The constant reshuffling among the regional and third-tier carriers did not seem to bother the public too much as the public benefited from reductions in airfares and increases in services, albeit with smaller and more economical turboprop aeroplanes in place of the larger turbofan aeroplanes.

The railway industry was not insulated from the wider impetus for deregulation, which had already progressed significantly in the United States under the *Staggers Act*, but the railway industry operated in an entirely different context from the airline industry since many rail shippers, including grain shippers, were captive to particular railways. The trucking industry could not provide economies of scale for the long-distance shipment of bulk commodities that the railways could provide. In Canada, railway deregulation ended much of the oversight provided concerning the rail line rationalization process and passenger-train discontinuances. Rates were made negotiable and could be implemented by private contracts instead of public tariffs. Regulation that had fallen into abeyance was repealed and the government transferred most of its regulatory oversight for rail safety directly to the industry. Nevertheless, there still remained issues involving captive shippers – those who shipped large volumes from locations where they could only access one railway and for whom trucking was not a viable option. The National Transportation Agency was kept busy dealing with those issues.

Although the *National Transportation Act 1987* did not affect the separate regulatory regime respecting grain rates, it did have a significant impact on the related question of rail line rationalization. The Mulroney Ministry, under which the legislation had been passed, remained committed to a public process concerning branch line abandonments but tilted the process much farther toward the viability of particular rail lines. The key focus under the new legislation was on the economics of the branch line operation, rather than the public interest (i.e., local social concerns). Indeed, consideration of the public interest concerning abandonments under the new legislation could only arise where the Agency determined that there was a reasonable prospect for a line under review being restored to economic status. Uneconomic lines with no prospect of reversing their drain on a company's finances were to be rationalized under the new statutory scheme.

The de-emphasis in the statute on the public interest aspects of branch line abandonment gave the new Agency latitude to dispense with oral public hearings in respect of rail rationalization proceedings. During the early years of the NTA, only one public abandonment hearing in the West occurred. In 1988, the NTA Chairman, Erik Nielsen P.C., a former Conservative Deputy Prime Minister, held a one-member hearing into the proposed abandonment of the CP Boundary Subdivision. The NTA Western Region provided some staff support to Nielsen's hearing and I attended it, along with the Western Region's Chief of Transportation Subsidies, Roy Proctor. The Boundary Subdivision lay along the border with the United States in British Columbia and the CP's traffic at this location was susceptible to encroachment by the Burlington Northern Railroad operating from Washington State. Most of the traffic consisted of lumber, and pulp and paper products.

The opponents argued that there were new resources that could be tapped and that traffic would increase if the railway provided more competitive rates. Further, they argued that retention of the rail line was essential for the future economic development of the region. While the sincerity of the witnesses who testified was not an issue, their assumption about the traffic levels was questionable. Nevertheless, Mr. Nielsen was persuaded by the evidence that the line had a reasonable prospect of becoming economic and that the public interest warranted its retention. He stipulated that the abandonment should be reviewed in two years. When the two-year review period expired the new evidence disclosed that there had been no increase in traffic and the line was abandoned, except for one small portion that was used for interchanging traffic with the Burlington Northern.

One of the major effects of deregulation was a change in the relative economic positions of Canadian Pacific Limited and the Canadian National Railway Company. In the regulated environment CN had remained a Crown corporation and one which had a public policy mandate variable with the times. The Canadian Pacific Railway was part of the country's largest conglomerate, Canadian Pacific Limited, which included a railway, an airline, a hotel chain, a telecommunications company, and an ocean shipping company together with certain miscellaneous enterprises. Canadian Pacific had always struck me as the more agile and business-oriented company although both railways were in the same league in respect of technical matters. Now, the government moved to privatize the CN under a former Clerk of the Privy Council, Paul Tellier. The CN began to grow its business and develop into an agile commercial player in the North American transportation industry by acquiring large American railroad assets. Canadian Pacific took another approach and unraveled itself, spinning off the constituent elements of the former conglomerate. By the early part of the 21st century the CN had become the dominant railway in the country while the Canadian Pacific Railway Company lagged[1]. One thing was certain about the deregulation movement and that is that it significantly

---

1. In recent years CP has improved its strategic position by acquiring the Kansas City Southern Railway, creating a rail corridor stretching from Canada to Mexico.

reshaped the relationships that had existed in both the airline and railway industries in Canada. The impact of deregulation was still being felt a quarter-century after it gained traction in Canada.

On January 1, 1988, the National Transportation Agency began operations and although the Canadian Transport Commission continued to exist for another two and a half months, the CTC Western Division began to implement the policies of the new *National Transportation Act 1987*, as the new NTA Western Region. Inevitably, a change of this magnitude had an impact on our position as a virtually autonomous Western transportation regulator. The arrival of the new Agency stripped away much of our former regional autonomy through the centralization of the Agency quorum and Agency program management in Hull, Quebec. However, in a large practical measure program autonomy continued. Since the NTA did not replace the Commission in law, it was necessary to both organize the new Agency and then to staff it by transfer or competition from amongst the former employees of the Commission, or otherwise. That process was more complex than it initially appeared and substantial managerial change did not begin to affect the NTA Western Region until after 1990.

Nevertheless, in 1988 our complement shrunk to a dozen or fewer and some faithful employees took their leave, seeking positions elsewhere in the public service or the private sector. I shifted from a formal legal practice model into a new position as Chief of Dispute Resolution, responsible for using alternative dispute resolution to resolve freight and passenger transportation problems in both the air and rail modes. My new duties also included responsibility for managing the Agency's western rail infrastructure program which often entailed site inspection/conciliation meetings with railways and municipalities in which I was accompanied by our regional engineer Henry Heinrichs (later succeeded by Shelley Hilkewich). I now found myself managing the efforts of a small NTA Western Region team of specialists.

Commissioner McDonough became a member of the Agency resident in Saskatoon but ill-health soon prevented him from taking any active role in the work of the NTA Western Region (Commissioner Wolfe had retired from the Commission late in 1987). In any event, the NTA Western Region lacked a quorum and could not issue decisions. Our office ceased to be a delegated regulator of western transportation issues but we continued to process matters for decision-making in Hull, Quebec. The government did not quite revert to the pre-1979 approach to regulation but as a halfway measure maintained a regulatory operation in Saskatoon that followed a program deconcentration model, as opposed to the delegated authority model of the former CTC Western Division. Primarily, this reflected a view by policy-makers in Ottawa that Western transportation issues no longer generated political concerns in Western Canada to the degree that they once had. In effect, the CTC Western Division had gone a long way towards working itself out of a role in regional transportation regulation. Officials moved swiftly to reintegrate decision-making into the Ottawa-based structures of the federal government.

However, there was still a perceived need for a strong Agency presence in the West, at least during the transition phase from the *National Transportation Act* of 1967 to the full implementation of the *National Transportation Act* of 1987. Therefore, in mid-1989, Kenneth Ritter, a lawyer and farmer from Major, Saskatchewan, was appointed to be the sole resident Member of the Agency in Saskatoon. While a single Board Member resident in Saskatoon would not be able to engage in decision-making through the regional office, he would be able to liaise with senior officials in the provinces and industry.

Ken Ritter came to the Agency after having served as the Chairman of the Saskatchewan Surface Rights Board. Where relations with the commissioners of the CTC Western Division had been marked by a high degree of formality, the opposite was present in our dealings with Ken Ritter. He was an open and gregarious individual who enjoyed wide-ranging discussions on everything from the development of prairie agriculture to foreign relations. Ken was also quite a wit and his humour flowed through our office. He became a friend and I thoroughly enjoyed working with him, as did everyone else in our office. After his appointment with the NTA had expired, Ken went on to become the Chairman of the Canadian Wheat Board after first being elected by his fellow grain producers to be a member of its board of directors.

Ken Ritter was the resident NTA Board Member in Saskatoon

Our main work continued to revolve around managing change to the grain handling and transportation system, and the management of the much smaller commercial air licensing program for small local air carriers, which was now substantially deregulated. In the mid-nineties, the NTA underwent further downsizing, and the resulting cuts led to the closure of the NTA Western Region office in Saskatoon in 1995. By then I had already departed, leaving in early 1992 to continue my transportation law practice by focusing on oil and gas pipelines, and electricity transmission, at the National Energy Board, in Calgary, Alberta.

EPILOGUE

The creation of the CTC Western Division in 1979-80 was an important development in the twentieth-century history of Canada's regulation of the railway industry. Change had been largely absent from the railway system in the West for several decades and the grain handling and transportation system was characterized by an entrenched stability. The freight rates for grain had been established as early as 1897, and branch line abandonment control had reduced branch line rationalization after 1932 and then froze it after 1975. However, the stability of the system had been purchased at the cost of deferred maintenance of the railway infrastructure, and it was inevitable that it would become progressively more costly to run the system as the eventual cost of rehabilitation of the lines loomed ever closer in time, coupled with the annual cost of providing operating subsidies to the railways. In effect, the grain handling and transportation system of the late 1970s had become economically unsustainable.

The conundrum for the government was how to permit the necessary structural changes and adjustments to occur through public regulation without unduly antagonizing the rural western populations who were electorally important to the major political parties? The solution was to establish a miniature version of the national transportation regulator and to give it delegated authority to make decisions in western Canada that took into account the interests of western Canadians. By creating a Western-based regulatory authority with Westerners at the decision-making apex, the Western populace would perceive the legitimacy of the regulatory decisions that were being made in the context of the Western grain handling and transportation system. The fortuitous sequencing in the establishment of this initiative, which was authorized by a Liberal Ministry under Prime Minister Pierre Trudeau in 1979, and then accepted and established under the succeeding Progressive Conservative Ministry of Prime Minster Joe Clark, before the return to office of the Liberals in 1980, meant that the concept of a CTC Western Division ultimately enjoyed a measure of bipartisan support.

The chance presented to me to act as legal counsel to the CTC Western Division was a fortunate one. As a young and novice lawyer I was given an opportunity to both witness and to help shape the evolution of railway law and policy implementation in western Canada during a period of historic change. I have always considered it to have been a singular and unique opportunity.

The eighties saw the piercing of the western cordillera by the Mount Macdonald tunnel, a final railway operating triumph for the Canadian Pacific after its century-long battle with the snow of the Rogers Pass. The ninety-year-old freight rates established by the *Crowsnest Pass Act* were abolished and a new statutory freight rate system was created that ultimately led to the establishment of variable freight rates for the carriage of grain. Those variable rates, in turn, signaled a rapid acceleration in the implementation of the branch line rationalization process. As part of the new rationalization process efforts were made to promote alternatives to branch line abandonments, including the first new short-line railway to serve the needs of grain producers to be created in many decades in western Canada. The Central Western Railway set a precedent for the creation of other short-line railways in Western Canada and in the country as a whole. There was also an evolution in historic portions of the western passenger train network during this period.

In the end, the creation of the CTC Western Division was a positive strategic initiative by the federal government. It helped to legitimize the greater scope given to the forces of change in the Western transportation system. One possible indicator of the success of the government's approach may be that when political churn occurred again in western Canada during the late eighties and the early nineties, leading to the establishment of new political parties and arrangements at the federal level, transportation policy was not one of the flashpoints of grievance asserted by western Canadians. Unlike earlier periods of political turmoil and change, the emotional context of transportation policy issues had largely receded into the background[1]. The CTC Western Division could not be, and was not, wholly responsible for that result but its presence and activities in western Canada during the 1980s significantly contributed to that outcome.

---

1. Although underlying economic issues and concerns will always be present.

APPENDIX 1 - THE GRAIN CAR ALLOCATION SYSTEM CIRCA 1980'S

For the reader to fully understand how the western grain handling and transportation system operated, it is necessary to review how the rail car cycling system worked during this period. The major responsibility for the movement of grain by rail fell on three agencies, the Canadian Wheat Board, the Grain Transportation Agency, and the Canadian Grain Commission. All of the western lines that carried grain traffic were numerically described as a train run by the Canadian Wheat Board. Those train runs were used by the Board in five-week planning cycles for the movement of grain from prairie origins to Thunder Bay in the east, Churchill in the north, or Vancouver and Prince Rupert in the west.

During the initial week of the cycle, the Board would determine which grains were needed for export positions at Canadian ports from the export contracts it had entered into. The grain companies would advise the Board what grains and grades were needed to fulfill Canadian domestic demand. The Canadian Grain Commission would receive requests from producers for producer cars to be spotted on a public siding.

During the second week of the cycle the Board would review the stocks on hand in the country from data garnered through the elevator companies from their managers at western locations. In the third week, the Grain Transportation Agency would discuss the available car supply with the railways and then split the car supply between Board grain and non-board grain. Producer car requests to the Canadian Grain Commission were also included in this split. Projected car allocation schedules were delivered to the grain companies during the third week. Grain companies would then decide where to allocate the car supply for non-Board grains which had been allocated to the grain commission.

For Board grains, the allocation depended on the grains and grades required, where the grain was located, and the availability of rail siding capacity at various locations. A formula was used to allocate the Board car supply to particular elevator companies located along a train run in proportion to each elevator company's share of Board grain business along that train run. Once the allocation for Board grains was made, each elevator company would determine at which of its facilities located along a train run the cars would be spotted for loading. The Board would then discuss its transportation requirements with the railways, as well as the minimum and maximum number of car spots that would be required on each train run.

In the fourth week of the planning cycle, the train runs would be executed and the cars spotted at country elevators for loading. Upon being picked up by the returning train run, the cars would be sent to their destination port. Sometime during the fifth week, the loaded cars would arrive at their destination port and the railways would notify the elevator companies which would direct where the cars would be unloaded. The Grain Transportation Agency assisted with the movement of the cars through the ports (a function which the CTC Western Division performed before 1984). The empty cars would then be returned to the prairies by the railways to recommence the cycle.

The allocation system was highly complex and depended on a great deal of cooperation between government agencies, the railways, and the grain trade in order to make it work effectively.

APPENDIX 2 - THE TECHNOLOGY AND RESOURCES OF A REGULATORY LEGAL PRACTICE IN THE EIGHTIES

When our senior counsel, Jean Patenaude, left the CTC Western Division in February 1982, I inherited his responsibilities for all of the legal advisory activities in the division. Essentially, I functioned as a sole practitioner in a government agency. As with any sole practitioner legal practice, my workload ebbed and flowed, with certain days being busier than others. A typical day would start with my arrival around 9:00 A.M. My first hour would be taken up with answering any urgent phone messages and dealing with the morning batch of railway crossing files brought to my office by one of our rail clerks, Karen Preston or Kathy Verbonac, after they had been seen by our engineer Henry Heinrichs and by the Director of Engineering Ken Tikkanen (succeeded later by Jim Cant). After I had reviewed the files, the clerks would submit them to the commissioners for decision-making. If approved by the commissioners, the formal orders would be taken to the Division Secretary, Randy Lebell, who would sign them following which they would be issued by mail, telex, or fax.

At midmorning, I would invariably meet for an hour or so with Jim McDonough, our Senior Commissioner, if he was in. After meeting with the Senior Commissioner I might also have a short meeting with Commissioner Wolfe if he was in. Since Commissioner Wolfe spent much of his time at CTC headquarters, I generally only met with him intermittently.

Early afternoon would generally find me in meetings, perhaps with our Director of Rail Operations Martin Lacombe (later succeeded by G.G. (Bud) Ripley), or one of our two economists,

Senior Economist Roy Proctor, or Economist Brian Gill. I might also meet with our rail traffic and tariffs specialist, Bill Elliot, and our engineers. Occasionally, I would meet with our Executive Director, John Kimpinski, who had overall administrative responsibility for the CTC Western Division, or our chief financial officer Maria Wall (later succeeded by Sheena Marsh). Our Division Secretary Randy Lebell would pop into my office at various times since his office was located next to mine.

In the middle part of the afternoon, I preferred to reserve for legal research or hearing preparation. I would walk down to the courthouse on Spadina Avenue to undertake legal research at the courthouse library or, more rarely, I would go over to the University of Saskatchewan to conduct research in the College of Law. If I was preparing for a hearing, I would work in my office reviewing the filed documents and preparing my cross-examination of the prospective witnesses. I might also use this time to work on post-hearing work or, if needed, I would devote time to appeals or reviews of CTC Western Division decisions.

Late afternoon was the period I reserved for reviewing commercial air licensing files which I received from one of our air licensing clerks, Natalie Postnikoff or Geneen Gross. These files were generally time-sensitive but straightforward in terms of legal issues and I usually dealt with them quickly. Sometimes, if there was a need, I would meet with our air licensing officer Brian Oliver (later succeeded by Shane Stevenson). Typically, my work day ended around 5:30 P.M..

The author at work in his office in Saskatoon, Saskatchewan

Technology plays an important part in the practice of law. First and foremost of concern is the adequacy of the physical premises. Here I was fortunate in that the CTC Western Division had acquired new, modern premises located at 350 3rd Avenue North, at the intersection of 3rd Avenue and 25th Street. The CTC Western Division leased the entire third floor of the building which provided ample space.

While the commissioners enjoyed large spacious offices with faux wood paneling, large, impressive desks, and comfortable chesterfields, coffee tables, and chairs, the senior officers were allotted much smaller enclosed offices with standard government-issue furniture. Junior officers were placed in open-concept offices while support staff worked mostly from open desks. My office gave me a good view of 25th Street and it was furnished with a standard desk, a standard credenza, and a standard open bookcase. I had a SaskTel centrex system telephone with multiple lines and buttons that would light up whenever a particular line was in use. The main advantage of this system was that it allowed me to determine if key people such as one of the commissioners or my secretary were already engaged in a telephone discussion. I could time my visits to them when they were free. An additional benefit was that the multiple lines made it convenient to forward calls between the different lines that were connected to my telephone.

In the current era the popularization of cell phone technology has made telephone usage ubiquitous but in the early eighties we were still tied very much to the traditional thinking associated with a land line system. While local calls were very cost-effective, we did not use long-distance telephone services unless it was necessary, owing to the expense of long distance calls.

In the early years of my practice, the main technology that I worked with was pen and paper. Our office had two secretaries and several clerks. One secretary, Wendy Kennedy, served the two commissioners and the legal counsel while the other secretary, Kathy Smith, served the Executive Director and the operational directors and staff. I would compose on pads of foolscap paper in longhand letters, draft orders, draft decisions, and reasons, as well as various litigation documents, and then provide my written drafts to Wendy Kennedy who would type my work. After she returned it to me I would review and alter the drafts and send it back to her for further revisions. This cycling of a paper back and forth between us could go through several iterations before I was satisfied with the end product. Needless to say, all of this took time and it was not particularly efficient. It was not until 1988, after our office had morphed from the CTC Western Division into the NTA Western Region, that personal computers were deployed and we could begin to capture the efficiencies that modern word processing technology allowed.

However, in the interim, our secretarial staff was fortunate to have been provided with an early word processor to supplement their IBM Selectric typewriters which eased their burdens somewhat in the process of revising typed text. The early word processor they used was known as the Four-Phase system and it was huge in comparison to the word processing technology of only a decade later. The Four-Phase system consisted of a large workstation unit that accommodated several very large floppy disks, approximately 12 X 12 inches. The units also had a large keyboard and a desktop monitor based on the cathode ray television technology of that era. A truly huge printing unit stood apart on a table and had a plexiglass cover on it to reduce the noise that the machine made when it was printing.

The printing technology was based on the dot matrix print technology of the time. Although the secretaries could save documents to the floppy disk that was not considered to be adequate for even short-term archival needs and therefore the disks had to be backed up at the end of each working day. That process involved the secretaries physically removing the floppy disks and taking them to a long, narrow computer room at the back of the office where the computer CPU resided. The CPU was about four feet high and ten feet long with traditional magnetic reels. The secretaries would insert the large floppy disks into a port and push buttons that would enable the copying of the data from the floppy disks to the CPU, where it was considered to be safe and could be retrieved again if needed. All of this was a slow and cumbersome process which is why the word processors tended to be used only for major assignments, such as formal decisions, while short letters continued to be prepared on the traditional IBM Selectric typewriters. The clerks responsible for the preparation of orders and licensing documents all used IBM Selectric typewriters when they prepared formal instruments. They took great care to avoid typing errors but if a minor error occurred they could correct it with typewriter correcting tape or liquid paper (commonly referred to as "whiteout"). Whether documents were prepared on a word processor or on a typewriter they invariably were printed on paper with a carbon insert to allow another physical copy to be simultaneously created for physical archival purposes. Those carbon copies were known as flimsies because the paper they were printed on, at least in the initial years of my practice, was a type of very thin, almost translucent paper. Those carbon copies were sent to our file clerk for putting away on the physical files of the Commission.

In 1985 we began experimenting with an early version of the internet, which was then called the ethernet. Through it, we were able to transmit large documents to our headquarters translation unit for translation of English text into French text. The ethernet system was quite complex, requiring several coding steps in order to send a communication. It was also quite slow, taking, for example, 20 minutes to transmit approximately nine or ten pages of text to the national capital region from Saskatoon.

Unquestionably the most significant technological change I experienced was the move to individual personal computers, which occurred in the 1988-89 fiscal year. The labourious process of drafting documents with paper and ink and then submitting them to an assistant to be typed and then returned for review ended abruptly. I now could compose my documents and revise them in real-time. This created a burst of efficiency and reduced the time required to handle files. Around the time of this development, I had changed the focus of my duties away from the traditional practice of law to a process of regulatory management and the application of the principles of alternative dispute resolution. Since my new administrative duties required me to spend more time with a file, the productivity enhancement presented by the personal computer was welcome. I quickly obtained a small printer to capitalize on these new efficiencies.

In the office we found that the roll-out of personal computers to all of the officers coupled with other changes meant that our two office secretaries and some of our clerks were now underemployed. However, the organizational changes brought about by the *National Transportation Act 1987* also gave rise to new operational responsibilities. We were able to offer retraining to our staff and most of them took it up and became junior officers.

Another important piece of office technology consisted of our telex machine. A telex was the modern descendant of the telegraph and essentially consisted of a networked teletype device. It allowed for urgent external written communications to take place close in time and over long distances. To use it one would compose a message on the machine's keyboard, insert the recipient's telex number, and then by pressing a transmission button the message would be transmitted over the network of CN-CP Telecommunications Service. The telex machine also allowed a convenient method to verify that the recipient's address was indeed the intended address. Messages received by telex were printed on green tea paper. It was a low-cost though slow system. We used it frequently in communications with rail and air carriers but it was also used for internal communications with other offices of the Commission. However, around the end of 1983, our office obtained its first FAX machine which allowed for typed letters to be sent over telephone lines to a recipient, and that proved to be a more convenient way to communicate. The greater part of our external formal communication needs migrated over time from the telex system to the fax system as the decade progressed, although, by the end of the eighties, we were still using telex occasionally, particularly for communications with air carriers. Telex services were discontinued as a cost-saving measure in the early nineties.

Our main form of communication consisted of general mail services supplied by Canada Post. Mail services were provided five days per week and mail moved in and out of the office every day. In our offices, we also maintained an internal mail circulation system by giving one of our clerks, Karen Preston, the task of emptying and filling each officer's in and out boxes once or twice per day. For urgent matters we did have a modern photocopier machine and multiple copies could be quickly produced and distributed.

Our office also had a large central area where government files were kept in open stacks or closed cabinets, as well as a small library. Both areas were the responsibility of our file clerk, initially Dorothy Rathie, who was later succeeded by Vi Sripaseuth. In pre-*Access to Information Act*[1] days, our main government files were divided into an official or public file, and an internal file. Since the Commission was a court of record it was required to provide some public access to its files under common law principles notwithstanding the absence of any general freedom of information legislation. It was my responsibility as legal counsel to review the official and internal files when a viewing request was made by a member of the public to determine if the material on the file had been correctly classified as belonging to either the official or internal files. Generally speaking, everything went on the official file unless the item was confidential according to law, or was a document generated for the internal use of the commissioners and staff of the CTC Western Division. I had to sometimes use my own judgement concerning some documents[2]. However, the subsequent enactment of the *Access to Information Act* simplified matters and thereafter I naturally applied the statutory guidance provided by the new legislation to determine whether legal access was permitted.

Our small library was equipped with some basic legal texts, including the three parts of the *Canada Gazette* (the federal government's official publication) for which we maintained an

---

1. Access to Information Act R.S.C., 1985, c. A-1
2. In addition to the situations where visitors came to inspect our files I also dealt with requests from solicitors for copies of accident reports prepared by Railway Transport Committee field investigators in Winnipeg, Calgary, and Vancouver. Reports were sought where collisions had occurred between trains and vehicles at railway crossings to assess the viability of a claim for damages. In such cases, I had to examine the reports to ensure that no conclusions of law were made by the investigators and that their reports were factual and did not contain prejudicial statements.

ongoing subscription, as well as an incomplete set of the statutes of Canada. It was rounded out with a selection of government reports and other documentation related to transportation in Canada. Fortunately, the Board of Transport Commissioners had once had a practice of giving to each member of the Board a complete series of the published Canadian transportation cases and one of the last recipients of that tradition had, upon his retirement, passed his set along to Commissioner McDonough. Commissioner McDonough, in turn, had brought that set with him to Saskatoon from Ottawa and I was therefore able to access the main Canadian reporting series on railway and transport cases[3]. That was the minimum I required to undertake basic legal research in the transportation field. I was told that the leading text on railway law Coyne's *Railway Law of Canada* was out of print but when I made inquiries about it to the Canada Law Book Company I found that it was still available, and I was able to purchase a personal copy which proved essential to the conduct of my legal practice.

Whenever I required access to more specialized legal resources, I benefited from the availability of the local library of the Law Society of Saskatchewan at the Saskatoon Courthouse. Jean Patenaude had earlier made arrangements for access by CTC Western Division counsel to the courthouse law library, and I was able to continue to avail myself of its resources during or after business hours[4]. The local librarian, Ms. Peta Bates, was very helpful to me whenever I needed to locate specific materials. The local law library had all of the basic materials required

---

3. The complete series consisted of the Canadian Railway Cases (C.R.C.), which subsequently became the Canadian Railway and Transport Cases (C.R.T.C.) and which was followed by two series issued by the Commission, the Canadian Transport Cases (C.T.C.) and the Canadian Transport Commission Reports (C.T.C.R.). A further series, the National Transportation Agency Reports (N.T.A.R) was subsequently created by the Commission's successor, the National Transportation Agency of Canada.

4. I also had a key to the library entrance to the building for after hours or weekend research.

to conduct efficient legal research and to note up Canadian and Commonwealth cases. With less frequency, I also used the library at the College of Law at the University of Saskatchewan, mostly when I needed to obtain American case law, or information on unusual legal topics.

Technology also played an important role in our public hearing processes. Our technological requirements were ordinarily met by contracting out for the required equipment. Our Hearing Process Officer, Louise Cyr, would take care of all our requirements from the rental of a venue in which to hold a hearing to the rental of any necessary vehicles, sound equipment, and microphones, as well as arrangements for the transcription of our hearings by court stenographers. The court stenographers used two types of stenographic processes. The older technology consisted of a shorthand typewriter and tape similar to what would have been used in a courtroom in the mid-century. The newer technology consisted of a mask that the court reporter would hold over his or her mouth and into which he or she would repeat the words being uttered by the hearing participants for recording onto a tape and subsequent transcription. On a lengthy hearing, we could arrange for daily transcripts which were subject to subsequent verification. For one-day hearings, we would only require a final transcript which would arrive within a week or ten days after the hearing.

The western part of the country overwhelmingly consists of Anglophones and thus there was no significant demand for simultaneous interpretation between English and French. Therefore, the CTC Western Division did not normally arrange for simultaneous interpretation of testimony between English and French, although it was provided for in the two variable rates cases. When it was required, it was obtained through existing government contractors[5].

---

5. There was no simultaneous interpretation into aboriginal languages except once for

Once or twice when hearings were being scheduled in a location in the west that was known to have been settled by Francophones the CTC Western Division approached local officials for guidance concerning the need for simultaneous interpretation. Invariably, the response was negative. One municipal official in Gravelbourg, Saskatchewan, explained to the Commission before an abandonment hearing held in that Francophone community that the local population contained many people who understood and spoke French but they also understood English completely and they would be upset if federal officials expended money on interpretation services that were not required.

Two of our personnel, Hearing Process Officer Louise Cyr and Commissioner Bernie Wolfe, spoke French as their first language and thus the CTC Western Division did maintain a capability to respond to Western Canadians in English or French. However, almost all our contacts in French involved French language media although some elderly prairie residents had been schooled in French, and on very rare occasions a letter in French would be received by the CTC Western Division regarding a matter that had been set down for a public hearing[6].

All of the CTC Western Division's formal orders and decisions were translated into French by the Commission's centralized translation services in the national capital region, and all formal orders and decisions were issued simultaneously in both official languages unless a matter was urgent, in which case the order or decision could be issued in English first with the French version to follow as soon as the translation was completed. Rulings from the bench at a hearing were delivered in English by the Commissioner speaking on behalf of the panel. Although I did not comprehend much of the French language, I made it a point to review all formal orders and decisions in both official languages before

---

Inuktitut which was provided during an air licensing hearing in the Keewatin District of the Northwest Territories in 1982.

6. According to my recollection, that did happen in one of the variable rates cases.

their issuance, and I became adept at catching some of the more common, or glaring, errors in either language.

Transportation was the focus of our work and since the CTC Western Division was a travelling board with an extensive geographical area of responsibility we used many different forms of transportation. Saskatoon was a medium-sized city with a compact downtown core so I was able to walk to most of my local venues including the courthouse library, and the registrar's office, or to make an infrequent visit to another law office, or the local office of a carrier. I also walked to the university on those occasions when I needed to use the law library at the College of Law. Taxis were only used when we were travelling outside of the downtown core, or going to the airport to catch a flight out of town.

Travel outside of Saskatoon to hearings in the Prairie provinces was usually done by automobile. Generally, we would rent two cars – one for the commissioners and one for the staff. Our Senior Economist, Roy Proctor, normally drove the commissioner's car while I would drive the staff car. Saskatoon was centrally located so we were hardly ever more than a day away from where we wanted to go. In some cases when it was a little too far to drive, such as the Interlake Region in Manitoba, or if our commissioners had a pressing scheduled commitment elsewhere that interfered with our schedule we would fly to a major city and then drive from there to our destination to expedite our travel.

Additionally, on a few occasions when our time was limited we would charter a small aeroplane from a local commercial air service, High-Line Air. We chartered a Beechcraft King Air, a small turboprop aeroplane with a pressurized cabin capable of carrying seven passengers. We flew the King Air into both regular airports as well as isolated, uncontrolled airstrips, some of which dated back to the wartime British Commonwealth Air Training

Plan. In heavy weather, a King Air could bounce around quite a bit in the sky but it always got us to where we needed to be.

Of the scheduled services offered by the major airlines I generally flew Boeing 737s of Pacific Western Airlines, or DC-9s of Air Canada, although I also flew in many other types of aeroplanes in western and northern Canada, including the Hawker Siddeley 748, Convair 580, De Havilland Canada Dash 7 and Dash 8, Douglas DC-3, Fairchild F-27, Shorts 360, Fokker F-28, and BAE 146. For one of the occasional trips I made to Ottawa for a court appearance or one of my infrequent visits to CTC headquarters, I would board one of the Pacific Western Airline (later Canadian Airlines) Boeing 767s, or one of the Air Canada A-320s, or A-319s (after Air Canada's DC-9s were retired from service).

I also made extensive use of the passenger rail network because I both enjoyed rail travel and felt that as the western lawyer for the national rail regulator, I should experience as many modes of transport regulated by the Commission as possible to fully understand the particular characteristics of each. At one time or another, I travelled on all of Via's intercity trains between Saskatoon and Winnipeg, Edmonton and Regina as well as on its flagship trains the *Canadian* and the *Super-Continental*[7], and its northerly services on the *Skeena*[8] and the *Hudson Bay*[9]. Once I even took the British Columbia Railway's railiner passenger service from Prince George to Vancouver in British Columbia and I was also aboard Via's famed Esquimalt and Nanaimo railiner service (the *Malahat*) on Vancouver Island.

---

7. At that time the route of the *Canadian* was Vancouver-Calgary-Regina-Winnipeg-Toronto and the route of the *Super Continental* was Vancouver-Jasper-Edmonton-Saskatoon-Winnipeg-Toronto. The schedule wasn't always convenient. One Thanksgiving Day I arrived in Regina aboard the *Canadian* in the early morning and had to wait the entire day in the vast but deserted public waiting room at the Via station in Regina to connect to the evening daily train to Saskatoon.
8. The route of the Skeena was Edmonton-Jasper-Prince George-Prince Rupert.
9. The Hudson Bay travelled between Winnipeg Manitoba-Hudson Bay Saskatchewan-Thompson Manitoba and Churchill Manitoba.

Rather less commonly, I resorted to the use of the inter-city bus system, especially the efficient Saskatoon to Regina inter-city bus service offered by the Saskatchewan Transportation Company. I also used the Greyhound Bus Service on one occasion in northern British Columbia when the schedule for Via's train, the *Skeena*, proved inconvenient. On several occasions, I used the Pacific Bus Line inter-city service between Vancouver and Victoria which travelled via the very efficient BC Ferry Service across the Strait of Georgia. BC Ferries' large comfortable ships moved considerable numbers of people back and forth between the mainland and the island.

In the eighties, both the CP and the CN still maintained ownership of legacy hotels from the heyday of their passenger train services. Particularly when I travelled by train, I availed myself of the amenities of the railway hotels when it was possible to do so. The architecture of the railway hotels was always impressive and I appreciated the amenities of the Hotel Vancouver, the Hotel Macdonald in Edmonton, the Palliser in Calgary, the Hotel Saskatchewan in Regina, and the Bessborough in Saskatoon (though both of the latter had been sold by the railways) the Fort Garry in Winnipeg and the Chateau Laurier in Ottawa.

The technology available in the eighties was adequate for my tasks. What I have found in comparing my practice of the eighties with the period of the early twenty-first century was that although the pace of work did not change over time what did change was the sense of being insular and autonomous as a professional. That has gone as a result of the explosive developments in communications and computer technology brought about by the internet and the ubiquitous cell phone technology, all of which have given our society a much greater degree of collective and personal connectivity. While there may have been less time for reflection as the profession of law moved towards the end of the century that was balanced by a greater ability to access specialized resources and information sharing. To some extent, however, the greater availability of information may have encouraged the growth of a greater degree of specialization, as professionals cope with the much larger inflow of information made available by new technology. The slower, more unplugged practice of the eighties perhaps offered one a greater sense of being part of a profession rather than an enterprise but one thing is certainly clear and that is that technology has become a major driver of change and adaptation in the legal profession. It will remain so for the foreseeable future.

www.ingramcontent.com/pod-product-compliance
Lightning Source LLC
Chambersburg PA
CBHW042047280426